Dark Continent
of Our Bodies

In the series

Mapping Racisms

edited by Jo Carrillo, Darrell Y. Hamamoto,
Rodolfo D. Torres, and E. Frances White

Dark
Continent
of
Our Bodies

Black Feminism and the
Politics of Respectability

E. Frances White

Temple University Press

PHILADELPHIA

Temple University Press, Philadelphia 19122
Copyright © 2001 by Temple University
All rights reserved
Published 2001
Printed in the United States of America

⊛ The paper used in this publication meets the requirements of the
American National Standard for Information Sciences—Permanence
of Paper for Printed Library Materials, ANSI Z39.48-1984.

Library of Congress Cataloging-in-Publication Data

White, E. Frances.
    Dark continent of our bodies : black feminism and the politics
of respectability / E. Frances White.
      p.   cm. — (Mapping racisms)
    Includes bibliographical references.
    ISBN 1-56639-879-7 (cloth : alk. paper) — ISBN 1-56639-880-0
(pbk. : alk. paper)
      1. Feminism—United States—History. 2. Feminists—United
States. 3. Afro-American women. 4. American literature—
Afro-American authors—History and criticism. 5. Black nationalism—United States. 6. United States—Race relations. I. Title.
II. Series.

HQ1426 .W465 2001
305.42'0973–dc21   00-053212

To Sade and Affie

Contents

Acknowledgments ix

Introduction 1

1 Black Feminist Interventions 25

2 The Dark Continent of Our Bodies:
Constructing Science, Race, and
Womanhood in the Nineteenth Century 81

3 Africa on My Mind: Gender,
Counterdiscourse, and African-American
Nationalism 117

4 The Evidence of Things Not Seen:
The Alchemy of Race and Sexuality 151

Bibliography 185

Acknowledgments

I like to tell my students that no one writes a book in isolation. My goal is to demystify the intellectual process for my students and to help them feel good about the process of having others critique their work. I am clearly an example of someone who has benefited from the efforts of a circle of intellectuals who read my early drafts and helped me develop my ideas. Because I cannot do justice to the character of the relationships that I formed with these individuals, I name them here alphabetically: Carollee Bengelsdorf, Corita Brown, Cathy Chetkovich, Cheryl Clarke, Julia Demin, Paulla Ebron, Ellen Eisenman, Marla Elien, Michael Ford, Evelynn Hammonds, Lynne Hanley, Ann Holder, Frank Holmquist, Kay Ann Johnson, Ann McNeil, Ali Mirsepassi, Nina Payne, Mitziko Sawada, Pat Haskins Sileo, Miriam Slater, Janice Tildon-Burton, and Barbara Yngvesson.

Many of the people acknowledged here have taught at Hampshire College, where I worked for seventeen years. This book was conceived at Hampshire and nurtured by the many colleagues, friends, and students I had the fortune to encounter there. I am grateful to all of them for the support and stimulation that they gave me during my years in "The Valley."

Dark Continent of Our Bodies

Introduction

Some time after my parents died, my brother Earl found in our attic an oral history of my mother's life. As part of a larger oral history project on older black people in Wilmington, Delaware, a student had interviewed my mother and then published the findings in a school publication. Few of the facts were right. The oral history told of a black woman who was fortunate enough to have married a professor and had the opportunity to rear their four children on a college campus. Well, my mother did have four children.

In fact, my mother raised us in segregated Wilmington, first in a largely working-class community that was being devastated by urban renewal and later in a "middle-class" black community on the edge of town. The "middle-class" community was actually economically diverse: It included teachers; a doctor; and members of the steady working-class, such as my father, James "Dick" White. My father's main job was as a postal worker, but he always worked at least one other job, usually as a handyman or "delivery boy."

The contrast between my life's experience and the oral history's fictional account has led me to think about the importance of life stories for the formation of black identity. Our families prepare us for life in a racist world by telling us stories or narratives that help us make sense of our experiences as black people. Although I do not believe this is the only way we come to understand race—the media, for example, also have a major impact on us—I believe that our family narratives play a significant role in helping us determine how to respond to our experiences.

The Making of a Race Woman

My family worked hard to develop strong black egos in its children. Every summer we were sent to spend a week or two with our paternal grandfather. In the 1920s he had been a follower of Marcus Garvey, and later he had been a founding member of the Afro-American Historical Society of New Haven, Connecticut. He had an impressive library filled with everything he could find on Africa and its diaspora. It did not matter to him whether a book was racist or uplifting; if it was about black people, he would buy it. It was in my grandfather's library that I first encountered both a history of the Ku Klux Klan, written by a klansman, and C.L.R. James's *The Black Jacobins*, a book that deeply influenced my development as a historian. I am fortunate to have inherited many of my grandfather's books.

At least one evening during our stay each year, my grandfather would tell us our official family history. I remember best the stories of resistance. He told about a daring escape north on a raft in the 1850s after white members of our family warned that the black members of the family were about to be sold illegally to the Deep South. He told us about his grandaunt, Affie Weeks, an Afro-Indian who worked in the Underground Railroad. My grandfather remembered her as an old woman who sat on the porch smoking a corncob pipe. My favorite story was about the relative who lost a leg in the Civil War. Granddad had a picture of him dressed in his uniform and holding his crutch. At one point he had to use the crutch to fight off a mob of whites who tried to keep him from voting.

My grandfather's stories were so wonderful that I began to believe that they could not be true. According to Granddad, our ancestors were free blacks as far back as the eighteenth century. In the 1850s, after they had escaped north, they resisted the slave regime through the Underground Railroad and the Civil War, and they fought for the right to vote during the imposition of segregation. These seemed like black nationalist fairy tales if ever there were any. But the more I learned about black history, the more I realized that these could have been true accounts of my history. Many blacks who lived in the upper South were free by the end of the eighteenth century. Tragically, a thriving slave trade in that region recaptured free blacks and marched them to the Cotton Belt, just as those who had been captured in the interior of Africa were marched to coastal areas before being shipped across the ocean. We know that Africans and Native Americans in Virginia often intermarried or had children together. My grandfather's Afro-Indian grandaunt Affie Weeks warranted mention in William Still's classic, *The Underground Railroad* ([1872] 1968). It would seem that I am certainly justified in writing this introduction as if all my grandfather's stories were true, as if this were my history.

Yet I no longer worry, as I did as a young historian, about whether these stories are true. The message I got from Granddad was that I had much to be proud of because our family had been part of the Resistance. In fact, I came to believe that I was to continue that tradition of resistance. The truth of my grandfather's tales is secondary. What is important here is that my grandfather *told* me the stories;

the stories made sense to me; and, most important, the stories made sense of the world for me.

A number of writers have pointed out that it is through stories—from the everyday to commercials to the meganarratives of states—that we make sense of the world. (See Hayles 1999; H. White 1978.) Without these narratives, we would be confronted with a bewildering array of disconnected experiences. Stories allow us to deal with forces over which we have no control. They give our desires meaning and make beliefs comprehensible and communicable. There could be neither religions nor ideologies without stories. My grandfather's stories were effective because they invited me to participate through my imagination. And his collection of photos further stimulated my imagination. The pictures of Affie Weeks and of my ancestor in his Civil War uniform holding his crutch stand out in my memory. By engaging my imagination, these stories reached my unconscious and communicated, *inter alia*, meaning, morals, and a sense of purpose.

Former slaves understood the power of stories when they wrote slave narratives and spoke on the abolitionist lecture circuit. Narratives were consciously designed to pursuade whites to join the abolition cause; the stories did so by creating a disturbance in the audiences that could be quieted only through the fight against slavery. Stories told by former slaves were the abolitionists' best mobilizing strategy.

Although white northerners constituted the primary audience for the abolitionist storytellers, black people formed a crucial part of their audience as well. Many historians overlook the importance of the black abolition movement in the North. But not all free blacks had firsthand knowledge of slavery, and many of the northern blacks who did needed the impetus to rise up against slavery hundreds of miles to the south. The narratives were just as important in mobilizing black resistance as in influencing white opinions. In fact, despite some white abolitionists' heavy editorial hand on the written texts, narratives played an important role in developing African-American self-image. Many African Americians heard these stories firsthand at the black abolitionist meetings that were held in the northern states. Narratives, then, were a crucial part of a counterdiscourse that spoke outwardly against racism and inwardly to the black community about appropriate behavior and worldview. In my 1990 article "Africa on My Mind," I take up the issue of the Janus-faced nature of counterdiscourse. I suggest that for whites *and* for blacks, narratives can serve to counter the virulently racist images of African Americans that circulate in hegemonic discourses. And, as I demonstrate in that essay and herein, in the process of developing a counterdiscourse, some stories are suppressed. Throughout this book, I consider how the suppression of certain stories and the careful crafting of others help regulate our social and political behaviors.

I also examine the way that narratives fulfill wishes and meet desires. I will never know, for example, whose wish was fulfilled in that oral history of my mother. Did the student invent my mother's story, or did my mother remake her own history? I no longer worry about what combination of desires led to the creation of that story. My mother had a strong desire to go to college. She was an extraordinary woman who had a lasting impact on the many young people she worked with when she became a teacher's aide late in life. The stories that I tell about Pearline Tildon White are a tribute of my love for her. I am an intensely loyal daughter; my doctorate was a gift to my mother. I scrambled to finish my dissertation so that she could attend my graduation before she died. I went on to spend most of my adult life living on college campuses and in university housing. And I have refused to marry. The relevance of this last decision will become apparent shortly.

My Story

I needed the armor that my grandfather's stories provided. I came from an upwardly mobile family that was poised to make a run for success as formal segregation crumbled. We were a typical family whose main breadwinner worked in the post office. My parents desperately wanted for their children to reap the benefits of the promises that desegregation appeared to hold out for African Americans. We followed the Civil Rights movement carefully, discussing its progression at the dinner table. My parents wanted to get out of the so-called ghetto. We discussed the pros and cons of the efforts of family friends who tried to move into white neighborhoods only to be bombed back to the black ghetto.

I suspect that my parents' longstanding dream of living in a trailer seemed a way to freedom. But they found only white trailer parks, and they knew we would be risking our lives if we moved to one of these. They finally gave up the trailer dream after finding a house in a largely black neighborhood at the edge of town. This, they felt, was a good, safe neighborhood in which to raise their two youngest children, my brother Earl and me.

The closest elementary school to our neighborhood had been historically white. Much to my surprise, my mother asked me if I wanted to continue to attend my old segregated school or transfer to the white school. I did not need to think about this. I knew that it was my responsibility to enter the white school.

From the start, I encountered racist resistance to my presence at the school. There was a struggle over which classroom I would enter. The teacher who taught the most advanced class was adamantly opposed to having black students in her classroom. She had declared her opposition to desegregation on the local radio, and she already had two "colored" students in her class.

In my corner were my former principal and my mother's best friend, Henrietta Henry. Aunt Hen was one of the success stories of integration in the Wilmington public school system; for many years she was its highest-ranking black administrator (Nutter 2000). With her intervention, we won the battle. Only later would I find out that we had lost the war.

When I got to the classroom, I saw that the students were divided into clusters. The two black students were seated in the same cluster with two white students. My teacher introduced me and asked if anyone wanted me to join his or her cluster. Fortunately, a good friend and fellow black student invited me to join her group. Thus I sat in the same cluster with the other two black students until I made new friends and moved across the room.

It seemed odd to me that one student sat by himself. I was in college before I realized that he sat alone because he was the only Jewish child in the class. To me, all white people were the same; I had no understanding of ethnicity or class. I had thought that the teacher just did not care for him. Only later did I realize that she was treating him as a descendant of the murderers of Jesus. In the middle of the school year, a fourth black student transferred into our class.

The teacher put her with the Jewish student. Apparently the teacher had no problem with mixing blacks and Jews.

I had thought that once I was in the class, the struggle would be over. After all, I faced no threats to my life or property, as had many of the heroic people I had heard about on the news. To me, racism came in the form of bombs and German shepherds. I was not prepared for the new kind of racism that was being institutionalized in schools—a racism that still reigns today—which was manifested by segregation through tracking, lip service to meritocracy, and disproportionately heavy punishment for small infractions.

Like many African Americans of the crossover generations, I faced barely disguised hostility punctuated by an occasional slap or public humiliation. I remember my art teacher singling me out from a group of giggling girls. She slapped my face and sent me to my seat, her words still stinging my ears: "That's what happens when You People come here. Don't you ever leave your seat again!"

I could not discuss this with anyone except my brother Earl. I imagined my mother's anger spilling out over the school and causing me further humiliation. Besides, I was having experiences that my parents had never encountered. The slap and public humiliation were the least of my worries. My sixth-grade teacher was setting me up to be tracked to the bottom when I entered junior high school the next year. I could not figure out why no matter how hard I worked, I could not seem to get good grades. I worried that my black school had not prepared me well enough, and sometimes I even worried that I just was not smart enough. But mostly, I blamed myself for not working harder. My family's intense drive for upward mobility combined with pride in our blackness helped shape my response to this new form of racism.

Even the realization that my classroom was not a meritocracy would not have helped me. There was nothing that could be done. We had won the battle of getting me into the best class at Lore Elementary School, but we had lost the war of getting me a good education. When I moved on to Bayard Junior High, I found myself in classes with a few learning-disabled white students and many black students with a wide range of skills. We were deliberately taught nothing.

Fortunately, with little understanding of the many forces against me, I felt it was my responsibility to my family and to the race to work my way back up the track system so that I could go to college. I read on my own and learned from my brothers and my parents. Clearly, my paternal family's political and moral beliefs created an important foundation that helped me make my way through public school without becoming completely damaged. They developed a counter-discourse that worked.

My Mother's Narrative

My maternal family had a somewhat different story. I learned most of what I know about the Tildon family from my mother. Pearline was a very ambitious woman who found few paths open to the upward mobility she so desperately desired. From her, I learned that segregation turned the brilliant sparkle of hope into self-destruction. Like the ancestors of my paternal family and those of many blacks living in Maryland, my maternal ancestors had been free since the late eighteenth century. My mother's family had come to own a significant amount of land, only to have the government take most of it as part of its development of the Aberdeen Proving Ground just after World War I. After being dispossessed of their land, the Tildons began migrating to the various mid-Atlantic cities, with major clusters moving to Baltimore and Wilmington. Many were grouped within a half-mile radius within Wilmington until government-sponsored urban renewal began dispersing them again. I remember that my Aunt Clara's house was the only remaining structure on her block as she held out against the government that eventually forced her to move to the new ghetto it had formed in the northern part of the city. I suppose that she stood firm as long as she could because she particularly resented being uprooted twice in her life. After the hurry to remove my aunt, her block remained completely undeveloped for over a decade.

The Tildons were particularly driven to retrieve their Maryland land from the government or to obtain a fair settlement. They invested heavily in education, which they believed would equip them for this fight. They became known as eccentric intellectuals. Still, most ended up in dead-end jobs. One cousin, for example, graduated from Howard University with honors but could never find meaningful work. She developed a kind of oddball, life-of-the-party personality and managed to live by her wits, often relying on help from relatives. My mother would take her in from time to time, and she explained to me that my cousin's way of life was a result of racist barriers to her success. But my mother certainly did not want me to follow in my cousin's footsteps. As my mother came to see her own ambitions as stunted by both racism and sexism, her stories about her generation became increasingly intertwined with feminist perspectives. Her story of her own life gained force in part because it was so closely tied to issues of race and gender. In 1929 my mother graduated with honors from Howard High School, one of only two black high schools in the entire state of Delaware. College seemed like the next logical step for her, she thought. But her family could afford to send only one family member to college at that time, and they chose her brother Hollis. Although my mother was very close to her brother, she felt that he had been favored over her because he was male.

Disappointed but not defeated, my mother sought and won a scholarship to attend a teacher's college in nearby Pennsylvania. When the college discovered that she was "colored," however, the scholarship was withdrawn. The injustice of it all plunged her into a depression. She fled to live with an older sister in New York City, where the only work she could obtain was as a maid. Finding New York difficult to manage on her maid's salary, she reluctantly returned to Wilmington and settled on marriage.

I learned many lessons from what Audre Lorde would term my mother's "biomythography." First, I learned that she saw marriage as a consolation prize. Although she loved and respected my father, a similarly ambitious man whose desire for a college education was no less intense than her own, she considered her decision to marry to be a sign of surrender to a life imposed on her by her race and her gender. Second, I learned that succeeding at upward mobility was a form of resistance. I was determined to overcome the impact of racism and succeed for my mother and for the race. Indeed, for me, my fate and that of my family became intertwined with the fate of my race.

Hazel V. Carby (1998) describes this process in her discussion of W.E.B. Du Bois. She shows how quickly autobiography fuses with "we, the black community" because of the experience of racism (30). Carby notes that, to make this link, "Du Bois had to situate himself as both an exceptional and a representative individual: to be different from and maintain a distance between his experience and that of the masses of black people, while simultaneously integrating his existential being with that of his imagined community of people" (30–31). My mother's stories about her family taught me that, however different or exceptional I might be, my fate was tied to that of all black people. The segregated, racist world kept our fortunes linked. As I suggest in Chapter 1, "Black Feminist Interventions," it is easy to confuse one's personal and class-based needs with the needs of "the race." My family prepared me for upward mobility by helping me construct my personal goals as race goals.

Carby is particularly concerned with showing the way that Du Bois was formed as a gendered intellectual. She argues that the needs of the black male elite became synonymous with the needs of the race. Much of my book is designed to expose the black feminist revisions of this narrative. Fortunately for me, my mother's counterdiscourse was consciously gendered.

Of course, there was much that Pearline did not tell me. After her death, I learned about some of the stories she suppressed. Most important, she left much unsaid about her mother, Sade. I knew that Sade had been a midwife and had delivered my two oldest brothers. My mother told me that Grandmom Sade had experienced bouts of severe depression and had often refused to leave her room for months. Yet her reputation as a healer and wise woman was such that she received many visitors in that room. Even as my mother told me of Sade's influence in the community and the trust that many placed in her knowledge of folk medicine, I sensed that my mother felt, at best, an ambivalence about my grandmother. I sensed that Pearline wanted to be the kind of mother that she wished she had had herself, and we did indeed become very close. I asked for more details about Sade, but my mother's stories were uncharacteristically vague.

Some time after my mother died, her only remaining sibling out of nine started to fill in the picture for me. Aunt Clara, then in her eighties, began by telling a story about a horse she had as a young girl. I had always loved her animal stories because she could make the animals seem to come alive. Suddenly, she spoke to me as if she had something to confess. It seems that Sade was a midwife who did abortions. She was arrested after a failed abortion that sent a young white woman to the hospital. My grandmother was fortunate to serve only a short sentence, after which she promised both the authorities and her children that she would stop performing abortions. But she was arrested again for performing an abortion on another young white woman. This time my grandmother served over a year in jail.

I do not know why Aunt Clara chose to tell me about Sade at that time. I was shocked to learn that my mother kept this secret from me. Now my grandmother's depression began to make more sense to me. I asked my father if he knew about my grandmother, and he filled in more details. These events in my grandmother's life had occurred when he and my mother were still in high school, before they were married. Apparently, my mother had been very angry with my grandmother for being arrested a second time. Both my father and my aunt told me that the arrest had mortified my mother, and she had created quite a scene. My grandmother had defended her own actions by saying she had always done abortions "down the country" without trouble and she did not see anything wrong with them. But my mother's desire for respectability was undermined by Sade's jailbird status, the sexualized nature of her "crime," and its link to white people.

So why do I tell a story that would humiliate my mother? First, I believe that, if she were alive, I could bring her not only to understand the feminist implications in this story but also to think of her mother as a heroic woman from the country who performed a service for women that the state unjustly sought to regulate. Second, I think the story illustrates the way messages can be passed along intergenerationally by suppressing certain narratives or by omitting key facts. In the case of the silenced story about my grandmother, the messages were multiple, including the need to be careful with white people and the importance of respectability around issues of sexuality.

Throughout the essays in this book, I interrogate the ideology of respectability that has motivated many African Americans, from black nationalists to black feminists. The ideology of respectability is one of a number of strategies that African Americans have developed to create unity. I am particularly concerned with the ways that we build political cohesion and form community by drawing too narrowly the boundaries of our (imagined) community. As I suggest in "Africa on My Mind" (1990), our efforts to form community often depend on the demonization of too many people. And as I demonstrate in Chapter 1, the politics of respectability are double-edged. Yet I do not want my writings to be taken as an argument that African Americans pay too much attention to racism. Racism is real and destructive; it needs a consciously political response. But I believe that a successful response needs to take into account the reality that African Americans are structured in dominance by class, gender, sexuality, and more.

Given this fragmentation, we often struggle over who gets to define the race, who is in the race, and what the meaning of blackness is. As Cathy Cohen (1999; Cohen and Jones 1999) argues, the failure to recognize that the boundaries of blackness should be expansive leads to inadequate political responses. Besides limiting the effectiveness of great thinkers such as James Baldwin, narrow boundaries lead to other negative consequences. For example, the homophobic tendency to exclude gay and lesbian African Americans from the black community weakens the entire community. Homophobia causes gay and bisexual men to feel compelled to keep their sexual practices secret, which allows AIDS to circulate uncontrollably. Also of great concern is the growing number of homeless gay, lesbian, and transgender youth who end up on the streets because they have been thrown out of their homes or harassed out of their neighborhoods. We cannot afford to lose these children.

This book tracks back and forth between a focus on the racism of the larger society and the narratives that African Americans develop to counter racism. As the chapters explore black counterdiscourses, they expose the ways that race, gender, sexuality, and class categories intertwine and transform each other. Categories such as race and gender are created to help the world make sense to us. These categories do not exist "out there" in the world. Rather, they are analytical categories that are always structured hierarchically and that have real consequences for real people.

This book explores the relationships between categories such as race and sexuality and the narratives we tell about ourselves. In navigating this difficult terrain, the book exposes the boundaries that we have constructed to create blackness. Boundaries are not bad in and of themselves. Rather, they must be constructed to be effective in the political arena. As part of our struggle, we must include the placement of those boundaries. And we must make the boundaries as elastic and expansive as possible.

Outline of the Book

The first chapter in this book, "Black Feminist Interventions," is designed to help people read black feminist theory. I have been frustrated by the tendency to read this body of literature uncritically. I think that black feminists will grow as thinkers if we engage each other's ideas more seriously. We need to put aside the beliefs that racists are looking for us to reveal our failures and that we must not evaluate each other's work honestly. I believe we are strong enough to withstand critical scrutiny.

In 1983, the editors of *Radical America* responded to my concerns and asked me to write a review essay of nonfiction black feminist writing. The article that resulted from that effort was "Listening to the Voices of Black Feminism." Because I remain concerned about the lack of critical engagement with black feminism, I have updated that review and given it a new frame as Chapter 1 in this book.

As with the earlier essay, Chapter 1 explores the intertwined relationships between race, gender, class, and sexuality and the black feminist probing of these relationships. As the chapter explores the rise of second-wave black feminism, it exposes the limitations of the hegemonic narrative that tries to convince us that feminism is an exclusively white affair that has little to do with black realities. Then the chapter turns to what black feminists have had to say about four common themes: the slave past, class, family, and sexuality.

The chapter as a whole examines the contradictory project of representation on which black feminists have embarked. It asks the following: Where is class in black feminist analysis? What is the relationship between middle-class feminists who are based in the academy and other black women about whom they write? What is the impact of sexuality on black feminist thought? Here and in other chapters in this book, I ask who speaks for the race and who gets to define the race.

In a book that focuses so heavily on African-American counterdiscourses, it is necessary to remember that not all discourses have the same power. Racists have greater ability to mobilize institutionalized power in this society than do antiracists of any kind. Chapter 2, "The Dark Continent of Our Bodies," stands as a reminder of the kind of narratives that circulate about blacks' and women's inferiority. It also demonstrates that the structure of racist thinking jointly constructs race and gender as categories of analysis.

A colleague of mine who teaches biology suggested that I read science, starting with Charles Darwin, in order to better understand feminist critiques of the life sciences. As it happened, I loved reading nineteenth-century science. Darwin is full of surprises. First, he is a wonderful writer of natural history. Clearly, as many historians of science have pointed out, at least some of his success is a result of his ability to write cogent and convincing prose. Second, although I had been led to believe that evolutionary biology (as opposed to evolutionary sociology) was free of racism and sexism, much of the structure of Darwin's thought was grounded in racial and gender prejudice. Finally, I was surprised to find that ideas about women and people of color were interdependent in his work; in nineteenth-century science texts, race and gender were constructed in relation to each other.

Chapter 2 is part of a black feminist effort to "talk back" to the scientists who have been so influential in framing a hegemonic and authoritative narrative that is both racist and sexist. Many black feminists have been captivated by the Hottentot Venus, a southern African woman who came to be known under, among other names, the name Saartjie Baartman. In the 1810s, she was taken to England and France as an oddity to be exhibited for profit under carnival-like circumstances. She eventually became an important "specimen" used by Georges Cuvier, the French naturalist and surgeon general to Napoléon Bonaparte, who dissected her in his effort to understand the "missing link" between man and animal. Her dissected body can be found in the Musée de l'homme where it was once a popular exhibit.

The black feminist response to this dehumanizing use of Baartman has come in many forms, including poetry, prose, performance art, and visual art (see, for example, Alexander 1990; Edwards 1997; Green 1994, 1996–97; Sharpley-Whiting 1999; and *Thunder Thigh Revue* 1986). I have noticed that we share certain characteristics in our approach to this topic. We use both hyperbole and understatement to distance ourselves from the pain we experience when we think about this story. And our ironic and sarcastic tones barely mask the anger we feel toward the scientists and carnival hucksters who exploited Baartman. I suspect that black feminist anxiety runs particularly high when we think about this case because so much attention was given to Baartman's buttocks. Too many of us are uncomfortable with our own African-like posteriors. It is as if we imagine that we ourselves are being led around by a rope for the pleasure of an audience of boisterous white men. Fortunately, a number of creative artists have managed to find some humor in this identification (see, for example, *Thunder Thigh Revue* 1986).

Chapter 2 places Baartman in the context of Darwin's argument that Africans were of the same species as, but less civilized than, Europeans. I find his efforts both amusing and depressing. He uses humor to describe the Hottentot Venus, but the joke is partially on him: I—a black woman and Baartman's figurative descendant—can critique his arguments. But I am saddened by the reality that his line of thinking still reigns in the popular imagination. Race is seen as "out there in nature," even as most scientists now believe that race has no biological basis. Even though we have moved into an era of gene splitting, biotechnology, and cyborgs, race remains immutable in the minds of most Americans.

Every three or four years, a new theory emerges that excuses discrimination and gives the scientific basis for supposed African-American inferiority or women's inability to lead. Books such as Richard Hernstein and Charles Murray's *The Bell Curve*, which we know help condemn many to lives on the margins of this society, come into mainstream discourses on race that try to force us into polite debates. Furthermore, black women's bodies remain the targets of institutionalized racism. In March 2000, the U.S. General Accounting Office (GAO) published a report about the race and gender of airline passengers subjected to searches by the U.S. Customs Service. The GAO found that "race and gender interacted" in such a way that "Black women were found to be 9 times more likely than White women who were U.S. citizens to be x-rayed after being frisked or patted down in fiscal year 1998 . . . [but] on the basis of x-ray results, Black women who were U.S. citizens were less than half as likely to be found carrying contraband as White women who were U.S. citizens" (GAO 2000a:10). According to the full report, in 1997 and 1998, black women were, respectively, three times and nearly twice as likely as white women to be strip-searched (GAO 2000b).

The GAO report did not offer an explanation for why black women were more likely to be x-rayed and strip-searched than white women even though they were less likely to be carrying contraband. However, it is clear to me that part of the explanation is the racist tradition of viewing black women's bodies as accessible to physical manipulation. Black women are strip-searched to reveal the "truth" of their genitalia and buttocks.

Black feminist efforts to reclaim the life of Baartman and "talk back" to nineteenth-century scientists must be seen in this light. This history resonates for us, because we remain under a regime in which our bodies are open to racist controls. Baartman's case causes especial anxiety, because her experiences represent the physical vulnerabilities that we still face.

In Chapter 2, I also examine the era in which science emerges as the authoritative voice on black women's bodies. I argue that nineteenth-century scientists often used race to explain gender and gender to explain race. And it was partly because these scientific narratives helped make sense of changing race and gender relations for Europeans and Euro-Americans that they became the authoritative discourse in Western life. I look closely at this racist discourse by isolating the intertwined narratives about race and gender found in Darwin's *The Descent of Man* ([1871] n.d.) and in nine-teenth-century issues of *Popular Science Monthly*.

In Chapter 3, "Africa on My Mind," I turn from the analysis of racist discourse to a consideration of Afrocentric discourse. This chapter is a revised version of an article that was first published in the *Journal of Women's History* in 1990. I wrote most of the original essay in Banjul, The Gambia, where I lived for six months on a grant from the Kidder Peabody Foundation. I lived in an exciting compound called Barrakunda, where people spoke many different languages and came from a wide range of class backgrounds. Living in this compound, I felt quite distanced from the nationalist texts I had taken with me to read. What I was reading seemed to have little to do with contemporary Africa. And I came to think that the texts had little to do with the history they purported to represent.

These thoughts led me to take a closer look at the texts to determine what ideological structures underpinned their arguments. Especially because what they had to say about gender in Africa seemed to have little to do with what I was seeing around me in Barrakunda, I wanted to understand in what ways sexism structured their arguments. At the same time, I wished to acknowledge the value that many Afrocentric narratives have in revealing the nature of racist discourses.

Since the first publication of "Africa on My Mind," Paul Gilroy's work on nationalism (1993, 2000) has had a major impact on our understanding of black nationalism. Much of what he has to say about what he calls raciology in African-American thought I find useful. Gilroy demonstrates that the structure of African-American raciology is like that of nationalist socialism in Nazi Germany. Although I find this argument provocative and illuminating, I believe that the differing contexts between the two matter more than Gilroy seems to suggest. As I argue in Chapter 3, lack of access to state power distinguishes Afrocentric thought from white supremacy, American patriotism, or German fascism. Moreover, Gilroy dismisses black nationalist insights too quickly. Afrocentric counterdiscourse is Janus-faced. Admittedly, much Afrocentric thought constructs narrow, sexist, and homophobic narratives that help confine black life. I argue, however, that black nationalism helps us understand white racism's impact in our lives.

What I find most distressing about Gilroy's work is that it contributes to the invisibility of the variety of black voices. He writes as if all African-American intellectuals are nationalists. This strategy may make his work seem fresh and unique to an uninformed audience. To those who know the range of black writing, however, it seems remarkably uninformed. I wonder why Gilroy is not in dialogue with nonnationalist voices beyond that of Henry Louis Gates. My own work has circulated in feminist circles for the most part; I do not expect that he has read it. But where are, to name just a few, Adolph Reed, Paulla Ebron, Herman Gray, Patricia Williams, Robert Reid-Pharr, and Phil Harper?

On one hand, Gilroy points out that African Americans are not a unified community and we should not pretend otherwise. On the other hand, he treats us as if our voices are not similarly fragmented. My goal in Chapter 3, as in the rest of this book, is to contribute to an understanding of black society as fragmented and to show respect for the variety of these voices.

The final chapter, "The Evidence of Things Not Seen," brings questions of sexuality to the foreground. I presented my first version of this essay as a talk at the 1994 Race Matters conference at Princeton University in honor of Cornel West and Toni Morrison. My intention was to help the audience think through the ways in which sexuality and race are intertwined in our thinking. Perhaps because the essay included a call for Morrison to take homosexuality more seriously, it received a mixed reception. Some people seemed offended that I criticized Morrison at all. Some of my comments were also misinterpreted as (1) being unsympathetic toward Baldwin and (2) using standards that emerged only after his death to judge him unfairly.

When it came time for the conference papers to be published, I was informed that my essay was "too personal" and it would be omitted from the volume. This charge reminded me of the dismissal of feminist critiques in the 1970s as too apolitical. At that time, raising questions about gender did not seem scholarly or political. Feminists responded with the now well-known phrase: The personal is political.

Clearly, my essay was transgressive. I had indeed used Morrison's ideas from *Playing in the Dark* (1992b) and "Unspeakable Things Unspoken" (1989) to read her own work and to reveal her tendency to escape from knowledge about queer life among African Americans. As for what were interpreted as criticisms of Baldwin, they were, in fact, largely criticisms of the circumstances around him that made him pay for revealing his homosexuality. In Chapter 4, I argue that there is a connection between African Americans' willful oblivion to queer lives in our midst and Baldwin's vulnerability. His life reveals what he showed us in his work: In this country, race and sexuality are inextricably linked. I do not take commenting on Baldwin and offering criticisms

of Morrison lightly. I have learned so much from both writers, and I owe much to the trails that they have blazed. I
look for the boundaries of their insights precisely because I
hold their work in the highest regard.

The stories that we refuse to tell, like the stories in my
own family about breaking unfair state laws, do matter. In
the arena of sexuality, we have allowed our history under
racism to dictate what we tell about ourselves. It is true that
racists have equated blackness with perversity and out-of-
control libidos. But the silence around queer lives will not
counter that racist narrative. Most important to me, it is in
this context of willful oblivion, as Morrison might term it,
that queer youth are forced into homelessness and an
increasing number are murdered for breaking with the politics of respectability. This book is part of a process of constructing new narratives so that we no longer bear such
casualties.

1 Black Feminist Interventions

Black feminism emerged at the juncture between antiracist and antisexist struggles. In this space, black women turned—and they continue to turn—their marginalization in both arenas into a vital political force. Too often, if this feminism is not overlooked altogether, it is treated as alien to black cultural traditions. At best, feminism is acknowledged in the fiction of writers such as Ntozake Shange, Alice Walker, and Toni Cade Bambara. But these authors have been in dialogue with a small, though important, cadre of women who have taken up their pens to construct the theories that have helped us understand the ways our society is hierarchically structured by race and gender.

In 1970, fiction writer Toni Cade (now known as Toni Cade Bambara) edited one of the most influential early works of black feminist theory, *The Black Woman*. This was a book that I carried around with me during college as a political badge of honor. It marked me as a feminist within the black student movement. In Cade's own chapter in that book, "The Pill: Genocide or Liberation," she describes an antiwar meeting in which gender and race issues rub up against each other. During this meeting to plan ways to turn black GIs against the

An earlier version of this chapter appeared as E. Frances White, "Listening to the Voices of Black Feminism," *Radical America* 18 (2–3): 7–25.

war, one speaker lists the *things* to be sent to "our brothers in Khaki" to attract their attention: "packages containing home-cooked soul food, blues and jazz records, Black journals, foxy Sisters who can rap, revolutionary pamphlets, and films." Cade reports that her guts cramped upon mention of "Sisters" (162). And she continues:

> Talk about being regarded as objects, commodities. Not one to sit on my hands, I raised a few questions about the insensitivity of that cataloguing and about the agenda in general, which nicely managed to skirt any issue of the woman's struggle or man-woman relationships. These remarks triggered off all around me very righteous remarks [about] "overly sensitive, salty bitches trying to disrupt our meeting with that feminist horseshit." (162)

The meeting continued with women assigned to kitchen duty, the phones, and typewriters. But Cade was not the only disruptive woman present. She recounts:

> And when a few toughminded, no-messin'-around politico Sisters began pushing for the right to participate in policy making, the right to help compose position papers for the emerging organization, the group leader would drop his voice into that mellow register specially reserved for the retarded, the incontinent, the lunatic, and say something about the need to be feminine and supportive and blah, blah, blah. (1970:162–63)

The meeting finally broke up when one male speaker urged the Sisters "to throw away the pill . . . and breed revolutionaries and mess up the man's genocidal program. A slightly drunk and very hot lady from the back row kept interrupting [him] with, for the most part, incoherent and undecipherable remarks." Eventually she shouted the Brother down

in gusts and sweeps of historical, hysterical documentation
of mistrust and mess-up, waxing lyric over the hardships,
the oatmeal, the food stamps, the diapers, the scuffling, the
bloody abortions, the bungled births. She was mad as hell
and getting more and more sober. She was righteous and
beautiful and accusatory, and when she pointed a stiff fin-
ger at the Brother and shouted, "And when's the last time
you fed one of them brats you been breeding all over the
city, you jive-ass so-and-so?" she tore the place up. (Cade
1970:163)

As a student myself in the late sixties and early seventies,
I certainly remember meetings like this, arguing with the
brothers, fighting with sisters we felt had sold out. These
meetings were one of the immediate sources of black feminism. Although a few of my sisters and I refused to be persuaded by the claim that black men needed to assert their
masculinity at our expense, to my horror, some of my class-
mates at the all-women's college I attended began to argue
that the time had come for black women to take a back seat
to black men. We had to give them a chance to lead—a
"privilege" they had long been denied. My incipient feminism railed against this position, and the emerging women's
liberation movement supported my stance.

Unfortunately, the seemingly authoritative view of the
rise of the feminist movement ignores such sites as Cade's
antiwar meeting and the similar resistance many of us felt.
This view presents the movement, instead, as stemming
exclusively from white women's experiences in the Student
Nonviolent Coordinating Committee (SNCC) and the radical New Left group Students for a Democratic Society (SDS).
In this scenario, black women functioned only as naysayers,
concentrating largely on racism rather than sexism, because

they never felt as powerless as did white women. In contrast, I propose that there was always a small but vital group of black feminists in the mainstream women's movement, and there were also feminists in the black liberation movement. I argue that ignoring the black feminist presence undermines the impact of feminism as a whole, and this willful oversight retards efforts to smash sexism within black society.

This chapter takes a critical look at the growing body of theoretical writing produced by black feminist intellectuals. The key task for these intellectuals is to represent black women in discourses on race, gender, class, and sexuality. In the complicated discourses surrounding structures of dominance such as race, black feminists both stand in for all black women symbolically and portray them for the world to see. As representatives, these feminists have been engaged in a contradictory project that not only obscures conflicts among black women but also destabilizes the meaning of identities such as woman, white, and black. In this process, we have entered the terrain that Carby (1987) has characterized as the quicksand of representation.

The first section of this chapter surveys some of the key moments and texts in the development of first- and second-wave black feminism and shows how race and gender have been interlocking and overlapping concerns from black feminism's inception. It explores the historical roots of black feminism and the context in which feminism reemerged as a conscious movement among African-American women. The second section focuses on four persistent concerns for black feminism today: the African and slave past, class, family, and sexuality. Intertwined with these issues are questions about representation: Who are black feminists trying to represent? How do they allow for differences among black women? Do they recognize their own self-interests?

I present this chapter as neither a review of black feminist writing—many important works are not analyzed—nor a complete history of black women's lives. Instead, I use examples that help illustrate the trajectory of black feminist thought and the issue of representation that I consider so central to its development.

Rereading Black Feminist History

To understand and appreciate the contributions made by black feminists, we have to begin by looking at the segregated feminist movement of the late nineteenth and early twentieth centuries. The study of black feminists from this period and some of their political positions has influenced the black feminists of today.

When black feminists look at the first wave of feminism, the problems inherent in forging alliances with white women are highlighted. Ironically, many white women, some of whom were in the most radical wing of the movement, learned the language and political skills to confront their own oppression through their work in the antislavery movement. Lucretia Mott, Elizabeth Cady Stanton, and Sarah and Angelina Grimké all worked toward the abolition of slavery and helped articulate the first responses to changes that women faced from the increasing separation of production from the home. Tragically, many of these early feminist crusaders, including Stanton and Susan B. Anthony, later denied the roots of their movement in the antislavery struggles and got swept up in the virulent racism of the late nineteenth and early twentieth centuries. Frustrated by their efforts to have women's suffrage included in the Fifteenth Amendment, they joined in alliances with blatant racists who worked against black male suffrage. Admittedly, Frederick Douglass's misguided approach of strategically placing black male suffrage above female suffrage (despite his commitment to the latter) alienated Stanton and Anthony, but this does not sufficiently explain their willingness to sacrifice the rights of black people for their own gain. Northern white women pushed aside old allies such as Douglass to gain the support of southern white women. And it was not beneath such feminists as Stanton to argue that white women should gain the vote in order to maintain white supremacy (Terborg-Penn 1978).

This betrayal stands as a harsh lesson for black feminists, and theorists and activists such as bell hooks and Angela Davis have been justifiably harsh in their assessment of this treachery. It came during the period when many whites were searching for ways to keep blacks in subordinate roles despite abolition—a point at which black people desperately needed allies. In those dark, postreconstruction days, black people faced new threats: death by lynch mob, virtual reenslavement on chain gangs and in prison work camps, and segregation enforced by Jim Crow laws.Racism lay so deeply embedded in U.S. culture that it appeared to ensure that African Americans would forever live and work under separate and grossly unequal conditions. In reality, however, the separation of blacks and whites required carefully thought-out strategies. In the South, the old elite who had held power before the Civil War used white racism to cement their political control after the war. Perhaps more important, capitalists in the industrializing South and the urban North were able to incorporate racism in a way that worked against the economic interests of both the black and white working classes. As revisions of African-American history have ably demonstrated, race and class oppression fueled each other (Cell 1982; Kousser 1974).

All over the South and even into the North and West, whites attempted to terrorize blacks into dependent relationships that would undermine their attempts to establish themselves as independent subsistence peasants. Legal measures, such as debt peonage and convict labor systems, forced blacks to work for whites instead of farming independently. Institutional controls over blacks were essential to this project, but they proved inadequate to guarantee a subordinate class; extralegal measures, such as lynching, were also required. Between 1889 and 1945, over four thousand African Americans died at the hands of lynch mobs (Williamson 1974:118). As the carnival-like atmosphere and public display of torture at lynchings targeted individual blacks, it also broadcast a loud, clear message to southerners both black and white: The races shall remain segregated and unequal.

A strong justification was needed to obscure the truth about this bloody suppression of African-American women and men. Whites turned to the very deep prejudices based on gender and sexuality to convince themselves that they had to suppress blacks and to rationalize the evil acts of both the powerful and the ordinary. As most black feminists point out, whites lynched black men, women, and children and rampaged through communities torching black-owned property all in the name of "white womanhood." The image of black men as savage beasts with an uncontrollable urge to rape white women resonated so deeply in the white psyche that even whites sympathetic to black people's struggle for equality accepted this myth as essentially true. Meanwhile, white women found themselves forced onto a symbolic pedestal that had little to do with their reality. As far back as slavery times, even upper-class white women had worked long and hard on both plantations and small farms. During the deep depression of the 1890s, they often labored without the assistance of servants. As Joel Williamson aptly points out, the southern white woman "found herself in the difficult position of trying to scrub the floor from the heights of the pedestal" (1974:103). Much of the hysteria about the "black beasts" functioned to keep white women in their place, even as the conjunction between the reality of their subordination and the myth of their fragile innocence showed severe cracks.

Today's black feminists have been heartened to discover that black women during the first wave of feminism clearly articulated a critique of the ideology underpinning the extralegal violence directed at blacks. Carby's (1985) study of African-American women intellectuals of the 1890s documents the penetrating analysis of three women—Anna Julia Cooper, Ida B. Wells, and Pauline Hopkins—as they deconstructed the relationship between race and gender. Carby demonstrates that the terms they use are strikingly similar to the terms used by black feminists in the 1980s and 1990s. The influential journalist Ida B. Wells provided an analysis of lynching based on very careful research that has yet to be rivaled. Carby translates Wells's analysis into the language of today's black feminists:

> Wells, in her analysis of lynching, provided . . . a detailed dissection of patriarchal power, showing how it could manipulate sexual ideologies to justify political and eco-

nomic subordination. . . . [She argued] that white men used their ownership of the body of the white female as a terrain on which to lynch the black male. . . . Wells was able to demonstrate how a patriarchal system, which had lost its total ownership over black male bodies, used its control over women to attempt to completely circumscribe the actions of black males. As black women positioned outside the "protection" of the ideology of womanhood, both Cooper and Wells felt that they could see clearly the compromised role of white women in the maintenance of a system of oppression. (1985:270)

As I suggest shortly, to be positioned outside the "protection" of womanhood was to be labeled unrespectable. Black feminists of the first wave understood the costs of this label to all black women. They did not miss the irony in the contrast between the fiction of black men's molestation of white women and the very real rape suffered by black women. Sexual assaults on black women perpetrated by white men continued in the postbellum period as if slavery had not ended; white men's maintenance of the right to possess black women's bodies had both immediate and far-reaching consequences. Bell hooks writes:

Sexual exploitation of black women undermined the morale of newly manumitted black people. For it seemed to them that if they could not change negative images of black womanhood they would never be able to uplift the race as a whole. Married or single, child or woman, the black female was a likely target for white male rapists. (1981:56)

Hooks could have added that the white skin privilege that protected most white women from black men left black women open to attacks by these men. Virtually no legal protection was provided for women who were portrayed as loose and licentious. Under such conditions, black women—promiscuous by definition—found it nearly impossible to convince the legal establishment that men of any race should be prosecuted for sexually assaulting them. The rape of black women was simply no crime at all.

Black feminists joined with other black women and men to protest their worsening conditions. Already accustomed to agitating for the end of slavery, blacks attacked postslavery oppression with renewed vigor. Much of this struggle was organized by and through black churches, the most influential of which was the National Baptist Convention, U.S.A., Inc. From its beginning until today, this has been the largest organization of African Americans of any kind (Higginbotham 1993:2). By 1900, women had formed the Women's Convention as an auxiliary to the National Baptist Convention. By the time this Convention emerged, women in the church had developed sophisticated analyses about racism and sexism. The Women's Convention focused much of its attention on the intertwined nature of black women's oppression. Influenced by the first wave of feminism, the Convention simultaneously battled against restrictions on the participation of its women in the church and organized against racial discrimination. Women integrated political discussions into their meetings on local, regional, and national levels. Yearly national conventions articulated the major political concerns of the organization's leaders, as they mobilized to improve the plight of black women in the black community and in the nation as a whole.

Closely related to women's work in the African-American church was the black women's club movement. Such leaders of the movement as Mary Church Terrell and Ida B. Wells saw the clubs as a way to mobilize black women to uplift the entire race. They also tried to establish links to white women's clubs, which often rejected them for fear of contaminating their womanhood. Ironically, white feminists such as Mississippi's Belle Kearney remained captive to the very notions about womanhood that kept white women subordinate. Purity of the white race was inextricably linked to the purity and safety of white womanhood. Failing as they did to recognize the pitfalls inherent in accepting separation from black and all working-class women, middle-class white women supported a system that traded a certain amount of power based on class and race for subordination to middle-class and upper-class white men.

Similar contradictions plagued the black women's church and club movements. The middle-class members of these clubs were more closely linked to poor black women than their white counterparts were to poor white women. Racial solidarity helped foster these links and kept the club members in touch with the needs of their less fortunate sisters. Yet what seems so clear to many present-day feminists was not apparent to the club leaders: the need to attack the ideology behind the good woman/bad woman dichotomy. They struggled to have black women reclassified as good women rather than expose the bankruptcy of the entire system. They keenly felt the injustice shown toward black women—they had few defenses against rape and faced great danger when they walked down the street alone or worked as domestics, yet they were accused of having loose morals. They felt personally wounded when their efforts to become "ladies" themselves failed in the eyes of white people. The black women's clubs worked both to introduce bourgeois customs to poor black women and to persuade whites of black women's ability to adopt these customs (Davis 1998).

In *Righteous Discontent,* Evelyn Brooks Higginbotham (1993) gives a sophisticated analysis of this dilemma. She speaks of this contradiction as the politics of respectability.[1] She argues that a politically active woman was consonant with a respectable black woman; it was her duty to uplift the race. In contrast, respectable white women were urged to avoid the public sphere. Thus, whereas white women's lives were constrained by a cult of domesticity, African-American women were expected to enter the public realm. The politics of black respectability included the expectation that black women would represent the race by fighting for racial equality.

On one hand, women in clubs and in church organizations used respectability as a discourse of resistance. By emphasizing the manners and morals of good black women, club and church women were able to counter racist discourses that used negative stereotypes to portray all black women as innately inferior. Higginbotham notes that it was not only middle-class black women who turned to this discourse; many among the working poor also found it a useful counter to racist narratives about black women. Both interclass and intraclass tensions were often fought out along the lines of respectability. Surely, one of the intraclass tensions must have been between men and women, as women sought to protect themselves physically in a context in which the state did not.

Ironically, by censuring African Americans who did not behave in ways that black club and church women considered proper, these women helped authorize racist stereotypes. In some ways, they worried too much about what whites would think of black people. As Higginbotham argues, "The Baptist women spoke as if ever-cognizant of the gaze of white America, which in panoptic fashion focused perpetually upon each and every black person and recorded his or her transgressions in an overall accounting of black inferiority" (1993:196).

Black club and church women also used the white gaze as a tool to regulate black behavior. As I argue in Chapter 3, all counterdiscourses are Janus-faced and contested. The politics of respectability was also a discourse within the black community, demanding the end of open expressions of sexuality and shows of "laziness." In this case, respectable black women spoke outwardly against racist discourse but also inwardly to build the kind of black community in which they wanted to live.

Today's black feminists could learn many lessons from this earlier flowering of black feminism. Earlier black feminists tended to focus on the difficulties of forging alliances with white women. The issue of internal antagonisms was largely passed over until very recently.

The Borning Struggle

Bernice Reagan (1979) has aptly called the Civil Rights movement the borning struggle, because it shook up U.S. society so much that it made way for many other liberation movements, including a revitalized feminist movement. In addition, since notions of race and gender depend on each other in contemporary thought, a major shake-up in one category has led to changes in the other. Therefore, to understand contemporary black feminism, we need to start by looking at the way that black feminism emerged from the Civil Rights and Black Power movements.

One of the successes of the Civil Rights movement was the establishment of black people's humanity. To accomplish this, the movement had to reverse the values in the binary opposition of culture/culturelessness that had grounded racism in the eighteenth, nineteenth, and early twentieth centuries. In this earlier period, racist oppression was justified in part by the belief that black people had no culture. Black intellectuals and activists have a long tradition of attacking this paradigm. One of the successes of the 1960s was blacks' revelation of a rich culture that others saw for a time as being superior to white culture in important ways. In a reversal of paradigms, black culture became a yardstick of authenticity for many radicals. (Now blacks are said to have culture, whereas whites have technology.)

As long as black feminist voices remained invisible, white feminists could be dismissed as lacking the approval of the authentic, black woman. Indeed, angry at the racism they had experienced from white women, many black women charged that feminism was foreign to black culture and participated in the silencing of black feminism.

The hegemonic or official story of feminism's second wave is correct in its claim that the feminist movement had important roots in SNCC. Most historians rightly emphasize the political skills and movement language that white women learned to apply to their own oppression as they worked on SNCC projects in the South. The official story incorrectly also assumes, however, that the expulsion of whites from an increasingly black nationalist SNCC in 1965 guaranteed that feminism would develop as an exclusively white phenomenon. Sara Evans, author of *Personal Politics* (1979), an early, influential history of the women's movement, follows white women into SDS but ignores feminists in the black liberation movement. In the popular and useful history of black women's struggles, *When and Where I*

Enter, Paula Giddings draws parallels to the nineteenth century: "Echoing the scenario of the nineteenth century, White women developed their feminism in a Black organization and then turned the thrust of their activist energies elsewhere. And as had happened a century earlier, the development occurred at a time when both the Black and women's movements were being radicalized" (1984:303). Neither Evans nor Giddings is particularly interested in the early rumblings of black feminism. Evans has nothing more to say about black women after whites leave SNCC. She follows the path of white women into SDS and ignores the black women who began to speak out about sexism. Evans's oversight is particularly unfortunate because it has played into a larger misrepresentation of the movement as appealing to white, middle-class women only. Not surprisingly, this view appealed to antifeminist forces in both black liberation and New Left camps. Feminist "personal" concerns were labeled petty concerns—after all, the war in Vietnam loomed, and black liberation was at stake. Unlike Evans, Giddings provides some details about the existence of black feminists as she tells her story about the estrangement between white feminists and black people. For example, she describes a conflict between the National Organization for Women (NOW) and the Third World Women's Alliance (a SNCC project led by Frances Beale) that concerned whether to take up the unfair persecution of Angela Davis at a 1970 march on Washington. Unfortunately, although Giddings demonstrates that NOW leaders tragically contributed to the alienation of black women by insensitively rejecting black feminist concerns, she tells us little about the feminist content of those concerns. We learn nothing about the Third World Women's Alliance except that it "was the only SNCC project still functioning successfully" (305). What an interesting fact that Giddings fails to probe: a black feminist project that survived the demise of SNCC!

Evidence of black feminism in the 1960s is difficult but not impossible to find. Toni Cade's edited collection *The Black Woman* is a wonderful place to begin looking. Its preface details many black feminist activities of the sixties:

> Throughout the country in recent years, Black women have been forming work-study groups, discussion clubs, cooperative nurseries, cooperative businesses, consumer education groups, women's workshops on the campuses, women's caucuses within existing organizations, Afro-American women's magazines. From time to time they have organized seminars on the Role of the Black Woman, conferences on the Crisis Facing the Black Woman[; they] have provided tapes on the Attitude of European Men Toward Black Women, working papers on the Position of the Black Woman in America; they have begun corresponding with sisters in Vietnam, Guatemala, Algeria, Ghana on the Liberation Struggle and the Woman, form[ing] alliances on a Third World Women plank. They are women who have not, it would seem, been duped by the prevailing notions of "woman," but who have maintained a critical stance.
> (1970:9–10)

The contributors to the book were engaged in a number of radical political activities, including SNCC, SNCC Black Women's Liberation Committee, black student organizations, and numerous black women's study groups; they also participated in more liberal organizations, such as the National Council of Negro Women and the Women's League of Voters. Toni Cade, Audre Lorde, and Alice Walker, among other contributors, would become better known as feminist writers in the decades that followed. Clearly, black feminists were active at the end of the 1960s and in dialogue with each other. No doubt, the early days of second-wave feminism were filled with alienating racist experiences. And, labeling it a white woman's thing, many black women were turned off to the entire movement. *But Some of Us Are Brave,* as one feminist edited collection suggests (Smith 1982).

Black feminists who look back on the late 1960s and early 1970s and see nothing but a sea of white faces in the feminist movement are often unconsciously emphasizing race issues over gender issues. As in many black liberation projects, here antiracism acts as a cohesive force, uniting black women across class barriers and muting conflicts between black women and men. Many see this cohesive force as a protective shield against racist persecution. Yet, as I argue in the final sections of this chapter, the contradictions arising from this unifying strategy can create their own troubling dilemmas. When we look at the black liberation movement, for example, we see many hours spent in angry debates over who should represent the race. Today's official nationalist story identifies the poles of this debate as Martin Luther King Jr. and Malcolm X, but battle lines were also often drawn along gender lines, as black women rebelled against the sexist assertion of black manhood. Many women raised questions about the meaning of manhood and how black people could redefine sex roles away from dominant patriarchal models.

Clearly, some black women experienced a growing alienation from black nationalism's celebration of black manhood. Considering the number of early black feminists who were lesbians, among them Audre Lorde, Cheryl Clarke and Barbara Smith, sexual orientation must have played a role in their alienation from a strongly heterosexist movement. Clarke has explicitly addressed the growing chasm between black feminists and black nationalists. In "The Failure to Transform: Homophobia in the Black Community" (1983), she argues that homophobia is a barrier to black unity and that ultimately black nationalists fail to liberate the black community because they do not transform its homophobia. Indeed, she accuses black nationalists of fostering that homophobia. Later (1993, 1999), Clarke analyzes her feelings from the late 1970s and early 1980s. She points out that she and other lesbian feminists, including Barbara Smith, learned from the Black Arts Movement to critique white cultural dominance while affirming black cultural traditions. She turns these tools on homophobic black male artists and nationalists.

No matter how alienated, however, neither Clarke nor any other black feminists would have denied that black men had been horribly and consistently oppressed in the United States. We were driven by the knowledge that black men had been imprisoned, mutilated, and killed in an effort to keep all blacks in subordinate roles. We knew that more black men than black women were likely to face jail sentences, chain gangs, and even the gallows. But the notion that black women were either complicit in their oppression or should pay for what white society had done to black men seemed, at best, a cruel and twisted interpretation of our history.

These debates took place in the rapidly changing circumstances of the late 1960s and early 1970s. Government repression was stepped up and served to splinter many active political groups, such as the Black Panthers. Black feminism, then, emerged during the height of the backlash against black liberation movements. The confusion that reigned in the wake of the government assault led many to escape into fantasy causes. Searching for easy solutions to our increasingly demoralized state, many turned to quasi-religious institutions, such as the Nation of Islam. The Black Muslims, as they were commonly known, did an admirable job of rescuing alienated drug abusers and imprisoned black men, but—perhaps in response to increased black feminist activity—the movement's leaders also helped lead the call for greater restrictions on women. The Nation's models of the family had little to do with black reality. Its petty capitalist leaders wanted women rigidly confined to a domestic sphere that was ultimately dominated by men. While I experimented with Afros and cornrows, my female Black Muslim friends in the Nation resurrected their straightening combs. They traded their pants for long skirts, insisted on bras, and asked permission to commute to and from work.

Meanwhile, other black women were joining cultural nationalist groups that placed the black family at the center of their programs. These groups, such as the Committee for Unified NewArk in Newark, New Jersey, and the Institute of Positive Education in Chicago, hearkened back to mythical African values to justify their misogynist positions. The appeal of such groups to black women totally escaped me at the time. Now, with some distance, I can recognize that the cultural nationalists had some good insights about racism, and, more important, they appeared to offer protection from the harsh realities of poverty and street violence that many women faced. Black men, although already dominant, were being called upon to become responsible for the financial support of the family, thus helping to lift a burden women had too often carried single-handedly. Cultural nationalists also affirmed aspects of black culture that differed from European-American culture, thereby asserting the existence of an autonomous black space. Indeed, their critiques of the dominant society threatened white hegemony enough to elicit repressive measures from the state. Nonetheless, their view that a conservative family structure provided a refuge from racial oppression blocked arguments for women's independence.

Frances Beale's 1975 article "Slave of a Slave No More" is a direct response to cultural nationalists and their self-serving interpretations of African history and culture. However, Beale, in turn—taking a position that stems from a variant of Marxism—is unfairly hostile to that African past. This view, which organizes human history into succeeding and increasingly progressive economic stages, sees precolonial Africa as a primitive place with backward social relations. Despite this unfairly negative interpretation of African history, Beale makes the crucial point that sexual relations in the past do not represent viable models for the African-American present.

Beale's article, along with such other classics as Toni Cade's *The Black Woman*, reached out to early black feminists as we emerged battle-scarred from our confrontations with cultural nationalists. We were trying to find a space, or an identity, from which to move. In particular, we wanted to recognize the racism that black people faced, without ignoring our growing distress over sexism within our communities.

The Rise of Identity Politics

To understand black feminist developments from here, we must keep an eye on the black liberation movement and analyze the role of black power in setting the stage for identity politics. The discourse of identity politics is closely related to the shift that came when the more radical elements of the Black Power movement challenged liberalism. Black power exposed the hollowness of universality. As good (or aspiring) bourgeois subjects, black students had accepted much of liberal ideology. In fact, they measured their deprivation in relation to the circumstances of whites in liberal terms, such as equality, carefully pointing out the distance between the liberal ideal and their own experiences. Black students were drawn to and exploited this society's shared meanings over concepts such as democracy, equality, and representation. But with the advent of black power, many became particularly concerned with questions of representation, broadly defined—for example, how blacks were represented in history and who represented them. We, as blacks, began to realize the extent to which we needed to represent ourselves and to address issues beyond our own particular lives.

This phase of the Black Power movement revealed the key idea that hegemonic groups represented only themselves, even as they purported to represent us all. In the feminist movement, a parallel insight revealed that mankind really stood for only half of human society. Subsequently, black feminists began to recognize that they were either misrepresented or not represented at all, and they worked to remedy this situation. They joined others in rewriting history, literary criticism, and theory. Along the way, they found that not only did the dominant culture misrepresent or underrepresent them but both the Black Power and the mainstream feminist movements also acknowledged them inadequately. Paradoxically, they discovered that black women had been carrying a burden to represent the race as a whole, even as they remained invisible. They began to develop their identity by contrasting their own experiences with both black men's and white women's lives.

Arguably the most important intervention in the evolving black feminist identity came with the 1981 publication of "A Black Feminist Statement" by the Combahee River Collective, a group founded in Boston in 1974. This group helped to stake out a place from which black women could speak about themselves by articulating their relationship to white feminists and black liberation organizations. And the collective asserted a common experience of sexual oppression as a constant factor in the day-to-day lives of black women. "Above all else," the group contended, "our politics initially sprang from the shared belief that black women are inherently valuable, that our liberation is a necessity not as an adjunct to somebody else's but because of our need as human persons for autonomy.... We realize that the only people who care enough about us to work consistently for our liberation is us" (212).

Combahee framed its political position in terms of identity politics. The group declared, "This focusing upon our own oppression is embodied in the concept of identity politics. We believe that the most profound and potentially the most radical politics come directly out of our own identity, as opposed to working to end somebody else's oppression" (1981:212). Perhaps most important, Combahee recognized that its members had to analyze more than one structure of dominance at a time, and they began to speak of the simultaneity of oppression. Black women did not suffer from separate oppressions but from interrelated oppressions. I quote the collective's now famous words:

> We believe that sexual politics under patriarchy is as pervasive in Black women's lives as the politics of class and race.

We also often find it difficult to separate race from class from sex oppression because in our lives they are most often experienced simultaneously. We know that there is such a thing as racial-sexual oppression which is neither solely racial nor solely sexual, [such as] the history of rape of Black women by white men as a weapon of political oppression. (213)

Combahee's refusal to prioritize either race or gender identity and the group's decision to stake out a particular space for black women was an important intervention. This insight led to a fruitful reconceptualization of African-American life, and it has influenced virtually all black feminists (Brewer 1993).[2] In essence, Combahee was asserting black women's capacity to take militant, collective action. The group's numerous activities are quite impressive. For example, the collective created a network of safe houses for women in Boston's black community and organized against police brutality. When members took up the cause of black female murder victims, their cries appealed to white feminists as well as to Boston's African-American community.

It would seem that white feminists might have considered themselves natural allies to black feminists such as those affiliated with Combahee. Surely, all were concerned about the interests of womanhood. Feminism had made all women more aware of themselves as women and had extended support to black women as they confronted the sexism of black men. And indeed, black women entered alliances with white women with the expectation that a raised consciousness of female oppression would lead to a constructive sensitivity toward other forms of subordinating oppressions. Not surprisingly, then, when many middle-class, white feminists turned a blind eye toward major class and race differences, black feminists felt betrayed. Some black feminists renounced feminism altogether, joining blacks who charged that feminism was relevant only to white women. Others, shocked by racism and a blatant ignorance of class bias in the women's movement, sought out an independent position that attempted to sensitize feminists to race and class issues. Indeed, much black feminist writing of the 1970s and 1980s called on white women to recognize the errors of their ways. This sentiment was captured by Lorraine Bethel in her prose poem "What Chou Mean *We*, White Girl?" which was published in the classic collection of black feminist writing *Conditions Five* (1979).

The work of black feminist Gloria I. Joseph highlighted the differing perspectives of black and white feminists. Joseph also demonstrated her commitment to working through these differences by coauthoring *Common Differences* (1981) with white, British-born feminist Jill Lewis. It is clear from Joseph's research that Bethel's poem struck a deep chord among early black feminists, some of whom had simply rejected the possibility of forming coalitions with white women. Many were just damn angry and justifiably so.

New Feminist Narratives

Some black feminists, including me, began to despair, however, that we would spend so much time in responding to white women's racism that we would have little time left for dialogue among ourselves. Frankly, I got tired of women who called themselves black feminists but had nothing to say about sexism. We had had much practice in speaking about and attacking white racism. It was much more difficult for us to figure out how to talk about sexism as we confronted racism.

A shift began around the late 1970s and early 1980s, as more complex voices began to emerge. One undoubtedly important factor was the increase in relationships between African-American women and other women of color. *This Bridge Called My Back: Writings by Radical Women of Color* (Moraga and Anzaldúa 1981) is a testament to these emerging relationships. This book, which was named after a poem by black feminist Kate Rushin and appropriately authorized by a foreword by Toni Cade Bambara, was edited by two Chicana lesbians, Cherríe Moraga and Gloria Anzaldúa. Asian Americans, African Americans, Latinas, and Native Americans all contributed to this edited collection. A range of perspectives emerged, and, perhaps most important, the authors were reading one another's work.

This Bridge Called My Back and the identity suggested by the term "woman of color" opened up new possibilities for African-American women (even as it created new contradictions by masking differences between various groups of color.) White women were no longer the only reference point for comparison. As coalitions with and more literature by other women of color emerged, we began to understand that our men could have relatively little power in the public sphere and yet dominate in sexist ways at home. Our men did not seem as powerful in the home as did many Asian-American and Latino men, who appeared to rule as true patriarchs, but these comparisons gave us insights into how sexism might be reproduced in our families with the collusion of our mothers and sisters. Moraga's *Loving in the War Years* (1983) has proven quite effective with African-American students, particularly her exploration of the mother/daughter/son triad.

This Bridge Called My Back and *Loving in the War Years* also reflected the fact that a new space had opened up in which black lesbians could speak about heterosexism. As I have suggested, a number of influential early black feminists were openly identified as lesbians, and the dialogues and debates among lesbians of color were some of the most fruitful exchanges of the 1980s. The work of Audre Lorde, perhaps the best-known and most influential black lesbian feminist of the 1980s, has spanned quite a range of topics and has blurred the line between poetry and theory. For example, her autobiography, *Zami: A New Spelling of My Name* (1982), did not make the unnecessary truth-claims of much social science writing. In what she terms her biomythography, she tells of her childhood in the 1940s and 1950s and her emergence as a political lesbian.

In *Zami*, Lorde interrogates the meaning of community. She poses these questions: Where is my community? Is it among white lesbians who could not deal with my blackness? Is it with the black female friends who pretended to ignore my sexuality? *Zami* is an intensely erotic book firmly positioned in the "sex debates" of the 1980s. Lorde argued strenuously for the importance of the erotic and open sexuality in women's lives.

The greatest impact of Lorde's work was her success in shifting feminist thinking from analysis of women in relation to men only to recognition of the complex tangle of differences among women (1984, 1988). Lorde points out that these differences often lead women to be at odds with one another. Lorde warned feminists to turn away from easy and fake sameness to embrace difference. And, finally, she was an activist as well. Among her many important acts was her 1981 collaboration with well-known black lesbian feminist Barbara Smith to found Kitchen Table: Women of Color Press. Kitchen Table's history, especially considering the short lives of most small presses, has been quite impressive.

The 1980s proved to be the height of black feminist intellectual output. Feminists continue to publish, but the sense of a radical movement supporting their work has dissipated. With some major exceptions, including Barbara Smith, most of us survive in colleges and universities.

Revising History/Creating Subjectivity

African-American intellectuals—broadly defined—have tended to detail the history of African-American oppression and African-American courage in the face of that oppression as a way to explain the present, to suggest political avenues, and to justify options chosen. For most of this country's history, the atmosphere in which black historians wrote was dominated by white intellectuals who tried to suppress our history. Our history was contested territory, and intellectuals struggled over the meaning of race, manhood, and citizenship.

Questions of representation were central to these struggles. As I have suggested, representation has two meanings: the act of symbolically standing for a group and the act of revealing the nature of a group. To represent is to symbolically stand for those who have no voice, on one hand, and to make clear the character of a group of people, on the other hand. Black feminists entered these historical debates seeking and offering representation in terms of gender and race. We found ourselves revising not only dominant history but also "black" history and "women's" history. In the process, we created a black feminist subject who had the power to represent herself.

The influence of black nationalist movements on black feminism has helped us recognize the importance of Africa in African-American history. Unfortunately, some activists, seeking to use African history as a rhetorical strategy to explain African America, have promulgated a simplistic and uninformed view of Africa. In *Common Differences,* Joseph romanticizes the African past by presenting African women as strong and powerful rulers. She does not question what the quality of life would have been for most women living under these rulers. And yet this evocation of the African past is an effort to recapture our stolen legacy, an effort important to us not only as black people but also specifically as black women.

Attempting to explore African women's history more extensively, bell hooks (1981) accepts at face value nineteenth-century accounts of African women as primarily beasts of burden. The complexities of African women's history disappear behind the issue of whether African women are strong or weak. In fact, African women's ability to control their labor and sexuality and to exercise power has differed greatly over time and place, as it must in so intricate and varied a continent. In precolonial West Africa (the area most closely and historically tied to African Americans), women, responsible for much of the farm labor and petty trading, banded together in organizations that represented their interests. These groups (secret societies, trade associations, and kinship networks) were structured hierarchically by age and ability. Although such organizations allowed women to exercise great power, ultimately men controlled the societies. My own research leads me to believe that in such societies where power stemmed from lineages and production was based in these lineages, men's dominant positions in families gave them (especially older men) greater access to power than women had (see E. White 1987b; White and Berger 1999).

However we interpret this past, we are really trying to understand ourselves. It is ironic that the images we project of African women are often as one-dimensional as many mainstream images of African-American women. Too often we look to Africa only for what light it might shed on us, with little concern for what African complexities might mean for Africans.

What is at stake for black feminists in the focus on our African past are basic questions about the source of sexism in African-American culture: Was precolonial Africa characterized by powerful women who lost control of their lives only when they became enslaved in the United States? Or were African women beasts of burden who continued to suffer in the United States? Was sexism in African-American culture a distortion of African culture imposed on black people during slavery? Or do we need to look beyond our white oppressors for the sources of at least some of the suffering that black women endure?

The origin and extent of sexism in African-American culture also occupy our attention when we turn to the slave era. All agree that historians have generally ignored black women in slavery. An early attempt to redress this imbalance was Angela Davis's influential work "Reflections on the Black Woman's Role in the Community of Slaves" (1971). This essay deserves an honored place in black feminist writing. Davis sat in her jail cell and, despite her limited resources, wrote a compassionate essay that spoke powerfully about black female resistance to slavery. Her own bondage no doubt gave her insights into a past that had become an analogy for the racial oppression of the 1960s. Her focus on resistance to slavery must have given her strength in the long days of her incarceration. Also at stake for Davis was the role of black women in the contemporary black liberation struggle. I read this piece as an angry counterattack on black men who could not accept black women as equal revolutionaries. "Reflections on the Black Woman's Role in the Community of Slaves" is not only an examination of racial oppression but also a vision of a community in which women would be equal to men in facing persecution and forging resistance. In both "Reflections" and her 1981 book *Women, Race and Class,* Davis demonstrates a keen sense of what it meant to African Americans to have their labor appropriated. Yet when it comes to Davis's analysis of the black family, her early work is flawed by wishful assumptions about black history. For Davis, the black family in slavery was characterized by sexual equality. "Within the confines of their family and community life, therefore, Black people managed to accomplish a magnificent feat. They transformed that negative equality which emanated from the equal oppression they suffered as slaves into a positive quality: the egalitarianism characterizing their social relations" (1981:18). Clearly black men never possessed the resources to maintain the kind of patriarchal rule that richer white men could. But black people not only created a strong family institution, as Davis suggests; they also expected men to head their families whenever possible. It is clear in Herbert Gutman's *The Black Family in Slavery and Freedom* (1977) and in my own research on rice plantations along the South Carolina coast that even many slave owners identified men as heads of these families. There was an ideological bond between slaveholders and slaves that placed men at the head of black families.

It is in the interpretation of the ideology behind slavery that Davis goes most astray. Her vision is blinded by her view of slavery as a labor institution exclusively—a view that cannot fully explicate the social relations that underlay this society. She quickly resolves the contradictions inherent in such a racist and sexist system. The question of how to reconcile the contradictions inherent in attempts to create such rigid categories as male, female, black, and white has always plagued U.S. social relations and created what can be called a category crisis. If "female" signifies "mother/house-wife," as Davis argues, then what does it mean to be a black female? If "male" signifies "patriarch" and "black" signifies "slave," then what is a black male? Davis answers these questions by arguing that black women escaped the restrictive definition of womanhood by being denied it and thus gained equality with black men inside the family structure. I suspect that, given the power of gender as an analytical category, no such all-encompassing resolution was possible.

The contradiction inherent in the idea "black female"— where "black" signifies "slave" and "female" signifies "mother or housewife"—is partially resolved, Davis's work suggests, by the bad woman/good woman formulation. Black women, like poor white women, were bad women. Yet in her discussion of Harriet Beecher Stowe's *Uncle Tom's Cabin*, Davis herself provides a case in which this formulation breaks down. Stowe elicits sympathy from her white readers for the important character Eliza by portraying her as a duly concerned mother—a good woman. Davis maintains, "The central figure (Eliza) is a travesty of the Black woman, a naive transposition of the mother figure, praised by the cultural propaganda of the period, from white society to the slave community. Eliza is white motherhood incarnate, but in blackface—or rather, because she is a 'quadroon,' in just-a-little-less-than-white face" (1981:15).

Ironically, the ideological contradiction between "black" and "female" left room for abolitionists to manipulate these symbols against slave society. The abolitionists demanded to know how moral whites could stand by and watch children be torn from their mothers' breasts in a society where motherhood was so highly valued. Abolitionists attempted to use the emotional appeals of motherhood and womanhood to soften the negative messages of blackness. Given the popularity of *Uncle Tom's Cabin,* such appeals persuaded a large section of the northern white population (see Yellin 1989).

Bell hooks also looks at racism and sexism during the slave era, but she comes to different conclusions from those found in Davis's work. For hooks, sex roles in the slave community mirrored those among the master class, because black men adopted "white sexist attitudes towards women" (1981:34–35). This position virtually ignores the development of a relatively independent black culture that shared some values with Euro-Americans but also transformed African values into African-American values. Moreover, hooks's view, like Davis's, underestimates the complexity of the interaction between racism and sexism.

Hooks's distortion of the slave era stems from her lack of or misreading of reliable sources. For example, she tells us that during the colonial era, because blacks avoided issues of sexuality just as their white owners did, slave parents failed to prepare their daughters to face sexual exploitation. Given the paucity of slave testimony and writing from the colonial era, I wonder what sources could have provided such an intimate view of slave interactions and worldviews.

Hooks legitimately points out that a sexual division of labor that favored men existed in the slave community. Both women and men labored in the fields. However, slave owners generally reserved the most prestigious and skilled positions, such as coppering and blacksmithing, for men. Women did most of the domestic labor, often after putting in as many hours in the fields as men. Yet it is likely that this division of labor stemmed from African values as well as Euro-American ones. Moreover, the existence of this division contradicts hooks's notion that black women were masculinized during slavery because they performed male tasks. Again, a one-dimensional attempt to explain the complex interaction between race and sex fails.[3]

When hooks points out the relatively privileged position of men in the slave community, she angrily castigates historians and sociologists for ignoring the exploitation of black women. Like a number of other black feminists, she argues convincingly that social scientists have been more interested in the symbolic emasculation of black men than in the actual rape of black women and, I would add, the actual rape of black men (see Chapter 4 herein). Too often muted is any sympathy for black girls and women left with physical and emotional scars. Ironically, discussions of the sexual exploitation of black women often center on the effect on black men's self-esteem and their loss of control over black women. Hooks explains, "To suggest that men were dehumanized solely as a result of not being able to be patriarchs implies that the subjugation of black women was essential to the black male's development of a positive self-concept, an idea that only served to support a sexist social order" (1981:20–21). Here hooks's acute sense of the injustice that black women have faced over the years helps to set straight the history of African Americans as mainstream social scientists have presented it.

Classic Dilemmas

Black feminist history helps illuminate the present condition of black women because it sheds light on such important feminist concerns as class, family, and sexuality. These three subjects, which are the focus of the rest of this chapter, often draw the attention of black feminists as they look at the contemporary scene.

The negative impact of capitalist development, which has created in its wake an impoverished and marginal class of black women, has rightly caused many black feminists to focus on the interaction of capitalist development with race and sex. Most black feminist theorists grew up in or surrounded by working-class families, and because of their commitment to black liberation, these women have not forgotten their less-privileged sisters. Although they share with many white feminists a healthy critique of the simplistic Marxian analysis that concentrates solely on class and capitalism (early Angela Davis is an exception here), they have been influenced by socialist traditions. The Combahee River Collective declared:

> We realize that the liberation of all oppressed peoples necessitates the destruction of the political-economic systems of capitalism and imperialism as well as patriarchy. We are socialists because we believe that work must be organized for the collective benefit of those who do the work and create the products and not for the benefit of the bosses. (1981:213)

In the now classic "Race, Class, and Gender: Prospects for an All-Inclusive Sisterhood" (1983), Bonnie Thornton Dill approaches systematically the oppressive forces in black women's lives. Although she would agree with the women in the Combahee River Collective that race, class, and gender affect black women simultaneously, she analytically separates the three systems to illuminate the ways in which they shape women's lives. Dill has focused much-needed attention on domestic labor—the only employment that most black women found available to them during the first half of the twentieth century. Not only did these women free many white men, women, and children from the drudgery of housework; they also gave many white men an illusion of patriarchy, complete with seemingly idle women and children. Then these household workers combined their hard-earned wages with men's low and often sporadic earnings to enable the black community to survive the permanent depression it faced (see Omolade 1994).

These household workers—invisible in most feminist literature as they were invisible in the households themselves—have many stories of their difficult lives to tell. In the 1980s, a former domestic worker, then in her seventies, entertained me with black-humor-laced tales about her work experience in the South and North. Each episode ended with, "I done seen some hard times." I also remember my mother telling me that, because of her previous experience with sexual harassment on the job, she walked home three miles in a blizzard (despite the protestations of her employers) rather than stay overnight at her maid's job.

Dill points out that black women were concentrated in household work because they were poor, black, and female. Their poverty limited their economic resources and educational opportunities. Their race narrowed their employment options to the service functions that grew out of their role in slavery. Their gender relegated them to household work, in a society where the sexual division of labor assigned to women most domestic chores. Since the 1960s, most black women have escaped household work, but too few have escaped to a better life. Now class, race, and gender combine to keep many in the growing underclass that no longer even has access to welfare.

During the rise of second-wave feminism, a new trend emerged among black women service workers: No longer were they all confined to domestic service or farm labor. By 1970, 32 percent of employed black women worked as white-collar employees, and 21 percent worked in sales and clerical jobs (Omolade 1994:23). A small but highly visible portion (15.3 percent) moved into the professions (53). Barbara Omolade calls this transition the de-mammification of black women in the postsegregation era. She argues that the transition has had mixed results. On one hand, many women gained access to public sector and/or unionized work. On the other hand, black women still face discrimination. In addition, the expectation that they play the role of mammy has continued; now they are mammies to the workplace and are expected to intervene in every crisis.

African-American women, like African-American men, have become increasingly stratified in the postsegregation era. Black feminists often experience this stratification as a form of alienation. The Clarence Thomas hearings, during which many black feminists remained hostile to Justice Thomas's nomination to the Supreme Court even as most of our black sisters transferred their hatred to Anita Hill, brought home this alienation. The African-American secretaries I knew felt that Hill had betrayed the race by airing her charge of sexual harassment in front of the entire nation. Not all secretaries supported Thomas, and certainly not all professional women opposed his nomination. There was, however, something in the spirit of this polarization that spoke to an increased class antagonism, even as it revealed a deep misogyny in African-American public discourse.

Most black feminists have had difficulty addressing this class polarization. Like their foremothers during the first wave of feminism, most have assumed that there exists an unproblematic relationship between them as black feminist spokespersons and most African-American women. In part, this assumption derives from the working-class background of many feminists. Dealing with the transition to middle-class status may feel dangerously close to accepting charges that we are traitors to the race.

Patricia Hill Collins's book *Black Feminist Thought* (1990) and her article "The Social Construction of Black Feminist Thought" (1989) represent many of the insights and blind spots of contemporary black feminist theory. She has read widely across the range of black feminist writing—*Black Feminist Thought*'s bibliography alone is worth the price of the book—and she uses the many voices of black feminism to "counteract the tendency of mainstream scholarship to canonize a few black women as spokespersons for the group and then [to] refuse to listen to any but these select few" (1990:xiii). She argues persuasively that this selective canonization of black feminists silences the majority.

In the process, however, Collins has chosen to impose a false unity and coherence on this array of voices. Interestingly, she has made the conscious decision to mute these differences. She argues, "When I considered that Black feminist thought is currently embedded in a larger political and intellectual context that challenges its very right to exist, I decided not to stress the contradictions, friction, and inconsistencies of Black feminist thought. Instead I present Black feminist thought as overly coherent, but I do so because I suspect that this approach is most appropriate for this historical moment" (1990:xiv).

I agree with Collins that black feminists produce theory in a hostile climate that challenges the very existence of our work. But by glossing over the differences among black women, Collins may actually be contributing to certain forms of class oppression. For example, despite occasional nods to class differences among black women, Collins sets up a false dichotomy between white women, whom she assumes are all middle class, and the quintessential black woman, who has "experienced the greatest degree of convergence of race, class, and gender oppression" (1989:758).

In part, Collins traps herself by creating a false dichotomy between Afrocentric and Eurocentric thought. This dichotomy forecloses creative and important discussions among black women. It assumes that the position of false unity is more powerful than the assertion of a more dynamic and expansive multiplicity. Finally the dichotomy cannot account for the impact of black culture on whites or for relations between blacks and other people of color.

Unlike Collins, hooks is well aware of class stratification and cautions us to avoid essentialized notions of black womanhood. She offers helpful insights about the traps of assuming the unified subject of "black woman." In her essay "Revolutionary Black Woman" (1993), she argues that essentialist visions of black identity limit the development of what she calls a radical black female subject. This limitation stems from a will to normalcy in which some members of the community monitor radical behavior. The guardians of appropriate behavior come from a surprising place: "Often the black women who speak the most about love and sisterhood are deeply attached to essentialist notions of black female identity that promote a 'policing' of anyone who does not conform" (1993:58). Many of these "cultural police" speak in terms of a sisterhood that enforces standards of behavior according to what the essential class position of black people is said to be. Hooks warns us that the standards of normalcy are often passed off as alternatives to dominant society.

When it comes to her own class position, however, hooks is less insightful. Unfortunately, we learn little about how her education at Stanford and the University of California at Santa Cruz or her teaching posts at Oberlin College, Yale University, and the City University of New York have shaped her thinking or experience. Her many stories about her family in the segregated past act as authenticators for her views on blackness and the world. This past allows hooks to assert with frequency that she is able to talk to black women across class—as if such discussions did not require conscious strategies to ensure communication. We do not learn in what ways different women respond to this highly educated and relatively influential woman.

Hazel Carby is one of the few feminists to address successfully this problematic between African-American women intellectuals and other black women. She is an Afro-British scholar who studied at the Birmingham Center for Cultural Studies under Stuart Hall and migrated to the United States in the mid-1980s to learn more about U.S. feminism. The first chapter of her book *Reconstructing Womanhood* (1987) spells out her early project very clearly. She has set out to write a cultural history of black women intellectuals by placing them in the context of the social formation structured in dominance by race, gender, and class. That is, she is interested in the ways that race, gender, and class articulate, or

speak to one another, and the ways that black women intellectuals of the late nineteenth and early twentieth centuries
intervened to influence this articulation.

In the process of examining these intellectuals, Carby
places herself within the larger black feminist project, but she
does not remain uncritical of this tradition. She writes a short
but engaging review of second-wave black feminist thought
so that she can position her own work. She begins this
review by criticizing identity politics as represented by Barbara Smith, a prominent member of Combahee River Collective. Although she acknowledges that Smith makes black
female and lesbian voices visible, she criticizes her for asserting that there is an essential black female experience and an
exclusive black female language. Carby argues that Smith
ultimately limits black feminists to simplistic images of black.
Besides seeing this position as overly defensive, Carby worries that this approach places black feminists on the periph-
ery, in a ghetto, without allies or alliances, a "precarious and
dangerous position from which to assert total independence"
(1987:17). Carby continues: "Black feminist criticism has too
frequently been reduced to an experiential relationship that
exists between black women as critics and black women as
writers who represent black women's reality" (17).

Carby then summarizes a cultural studies intervention
into black feminist theory. First, she builds on Mikhail
Bakhtin's insights to argue that language is a terrain of
power relations and that the study of language can reveal
"the nature of one particular group" (1987:17). For Carby,
the study of black women's language reveals not only differences between black and white women but also differences among black women. Second, she calls on Stuart
Hall's theoretical writings to explore the ways that societies

are structured in dominance by class and race—and, she adds, by gender. Here she sees race and gender ideologies as serving the interest of the dominant classes.

Carby gives us helpful tools for understanding the heterogeneity of black women's experiences, as she illuminates the relationships between race, gender, and class. In a more recent book, *Race Men* (1998), she courageously turns her gaze toward black male intellectuals. Very few black feminist intellectuals have been willing to call black male intellectuals on the sexist structures of their arguments and behavior. Carby, in contrast, is particularly hard on the tendency for these male intellectuals to speak for the race without problematizing their position as men and as intellectuals.

When it comes to what Carby has to say about black feminists, I would add some understanding of why black female intellectuals may fall into an essentialist trap of assuming a unified experience for all black women. That there are class tensions among black women is not surprising, but the substance of this class antagonism has much to do with the fact that feminist discourse is accused of being white dominated. It is the desire for authenticity and acceptance by the black community that prompts so many black feminist intellectuals to try to obscure their class positions. Many, like bell hooks, have a genuine desire to identify with our poorer mothers and sisters; and many, such as Patricia Hill Collins, purposefully mute differences as a strategy for creating safe spaces from which to move politically. Perhaps most important, we know that we are threatened with a kind of racial excommunication for exposing the internal tensions caused by sexism. In this period of heightened racism, excommunication is no laughing matter. Unfortunately, our denial of class differences will doom us to a false unity that will suppress as much as it liberates. We need to find a way to listen to the opinions held by nonfeminist black women without delegitimizing our own voices.

The Black Family and Its Contradictions

Carby's "White Woman Listen! Black Feminism and the Boundaries of Sisterhood" (first published in 1982 before Carby migrated to the United States) identifies a central contradiction in the black family that makes the task of black feminist theory difficult:

> We would not seek to deny that the family can be a source of oppression for us but we also wish to examine how the black family has functioned as a prime source of resistance to oppression. We need to recognize that during slavery, periods of colonization, and under the present authoritarian state, the black family has been a site of political and cultural resistance to racism. (69–70)

Moreover, the black family has in its very structure even deeper contradictions. The establishment of the family during slavery, for example, can be viewed both as an act of defiance (as an institution in which slaves actively and forcefully created their own space) and an act of accommodation (as an institution that bound African Americans to the slave system).

Barbara Omolade (1994) faces these contradictions squarely in her discussion of black single mothers, the women who have helped reproduce our families during this period of serious economic and political decline. She writes movingly and perceptively about these mothers, noting both their trials and triumphs. She traverses dangerous territory here; black single mothers are maligned by the mass media as well as in mainstream and nationalist black discourse. "Commonsense" arguments often mistakenly assert that single black mothers are the cause of black poverty rather than a creative and much-needed response to poverty and virtual disenfranchisement.

Whereas most people think the problem with many of these families is a lack of men, Omolade sees their major problem as lack of money (1994:71). This confusion often underpins welfare policies, many of which "confuse the economic issue of how to support a family with the personal issues of sexuality and procreation" (71). Contrary to much popular opinion, most single black mothers are not solely dependent on welfare but either combine welfare with work or are counted fully among the working poor. Although material resources are often limited for women in a society filled with sex discrimination, a growing number of single black women are stable, working, and middle class. Like poor women, they become heads of households because they never married, are divorced, or are widowed. Many have escaped violent or abusive relationships.

Omolade argues that the scapegoating of black single mothers obscures both the realities of many low-income women's lives and this society's lack of commitment to children's welfare and progressive social policies. Bringing understanding to their lives is not easy, however. Of this dilemma, she writes:

> The scapegoating of Black single mothers makes it hard to honestly discuss the families of poor and working class Black people. If we criticize the welfare system, we give ammunition to an administration bent on dismantling welfare. If we attack Black male chauvinism, our remarks add to the undermining of young and working class Black men. If we

criticize Black women's participation in their own "sweet suffering," we reinforce those who deny the reality of Black female oppression or disparage Black women's competence. If we speak in public, we are accused of adding to white racist self-fulfilling prophecies of Black failure. Yet, if we are silent about the weaknesses in Black families, keeping Black male violence and failure in the closet, we risk further abuse of Black women and children. (1994:77)

Like Carby, Omolade has identified one of the major dilemmas faced by black feminist intellectuals. Most recognize the disastrous attack by the state on black men. For many of us, the central dilemma is how to articulate a feminist position without colluding in dominant society's further persecution of black men. Yet too many of us face male violence alone, without community support.

Beth Richie has developed a powerful black feminist voice for speaking out against domestic violence. As cochair of the Women of Color Task Force of the National Coalition against Domestic Violence during the 1980s, Richie (who at that time was known as Beth Richie-Bush) began organizing in the black and Latino communities with the intention of assisting families in their fight against racist oppression. Soon, however, it became apparent to Richie that these families had serious internal problems that threatened the lives of black women and Latinas:

After a period of time, I gradually realized that some of these strong, culturally-identified families, which we had been supporting so vehemently, were dangerous places for some women to live. Furthermore, the political machine at the forefront of the grass-roots community movement was in fact subtly exploiting women by denying the reality of sexual oppression. As I began to look closely, the incidents of battering, rape and sexual harassment became obvious. (Richie-Bush 1983:16)

Yet Richie felt trapped by the fear that the African-American and Latino communities would accuse her of disloyalty if she spoke out against battering and sexual abuse in a community under siege from racial and economic oppression. Eventually she found her voice to protest domestic violence by giving the women among whom she worked the space to bring out issues that were important to them. The problem of domestic violence naturally emerged during this process, and served, as it has for many black women, as a path into feminist consciousness.

More recently, Richie (1996) has used the concept of gender entrapment to explore the ways that many poor black women end up imprisoned. In a study of Rikers Island, she argues that many of the women who end up at that prison are entrapped by their race, gender, and class. In their attempt to live up to community standards of appropriate gender behavior, they turn to crime. Richie's logic is in direct contrast to dominant commonsense judgments of these women as simply irresponsible drug addicts and bad mothers:

> Violence by their intimate partners created chaos in their lives. . . . Racism furthered the impact of violence and influenced the sense of loyalty to the men who battered them and adherence to the cultural values regarding gender and roles and relationships. Poverty seriously limited the options the African American women felt in response to the intimate and systematic abuse. . . . This, combined with their aspirations of success, their invisibility to human service programs, and more aggressive criminal justice policies compelled the African American battered women to crime. (1996:159–60)

Richie's analysis is complex in that it takes into account both racism in the dominant culture and sexism in African-American culture and families. The women she studied are trapped by narrow black politics that prevent them from using the state to protect themselves from their batterers and trampled by out-of-control anticrime operations in communities of color.

Few studies of the black family pay much attention to mother/daughter relations. Gloria Joseph's work (1981) stands as a much-needed challenge to this tradition. It insists that race intervenes in the mothering process and that, in order to be understood, the black mother/daughter dyad must be placed within the context of this racist society. For example, black mothers teach their daughters not only how to survive within the black community but also how to continue the survival of the black community itself. Joseph argues that, historically, black mothers and daughters have been subject to conditions different from those of white mothers and daughters.

Although Joseph argues that mothers are more valued in black culture than in Euro-American cultures, she is aware of the contradictions inherent in the celebration of black motherhood:

> The Black mother, however, is also a woman, and herein lies the great contradiction. The "honored" mother is the same second-class citizen who is often regarded and treated as an object to be used, bruised, and abused for years and who is considered to be used up after thirty, forty, or forty-five years. The societal attitude toward Mother is one of both idealization and degradation. The mother's role in the family is symbolic of contradictions and contrasts.
> (1981:92)

As black women fulfill this unique role, they socialize their daughters to become independent beings who nevertheless define themselves in relationship to men.

Insights from white feminists, even when they have been color-blind, can help us understand these contradictions. Nancy Chodorow and Susan Contralto (1982) have examined the literature on mothering and noted the strong tendency to portray mothers as all-powerful creatures responsible for the psychological health or illness of children. There are only good mothers and bad mothers, just as there are only good girls and bad girls. Indeed, Joseph's work itself has the regrettable tendency to fall into this kind of thinking. Her black mothers are strong black women: good mothers.

Mothers loom like giants in the lives of most women. We all face the psychological struggles involved in trimming these giants down to human proportions. This task is made particularly difficult for black women, because we so identify with our mothers' struggles. Many of us have mothers who persevered through hard times; an increasing number of us have mothers who raised us alone. Despite their good efforts, our mothers face many negative images in this society. How dare we admit the psychological battles that need to be fought with the very women who taught us how to survive in this racist and sexist world? We would feel like ungrateful traitors if we did so.

The dilemma facing black feminists who want to reach a balanced understanding of black mothering is great. Yet, as feminists, we must struggle with this dilemma if we are to break the bonds that hold us in sexist relationships. As Gloria Joseph so rightly points out, many black mothers teach their daughters to expect sexist behavior from black men, and many women remain trapped in abusive families. We need to understand the role that mothers play in socializing women into both accepting and resisting these relationships.

It is within the family, along with other key institutions such as schools and the media, that black women are social-ized to seek out and remain in heterosexual relationships that are often abusive. Moreover, black women are not taught to challenge black men on their sexism. Instead, women are offered tools to help them persevere when men withdraw from their part in the collective responsibility for the family or remain present but abusive. The black family has evolved into an institution that offers shelter for the black community in the face of political repression and eco-nomic depression. Unfortunately, black women continue to pay the heaviest toll for keeping this shelter together—a fact that will go unrecognized as long as black feminists focus only on the positive aspects of the black family and ignore the power imbalance that favors men.

Sexuality and Representation

Barbara Omolade argues that there has been "a profound and disturbing decline in the quality of the Black hetero-sexual experiences" over the past couple of decades. She relates this decline to a sexual liberation that makes sexual-ity casual and public in a male chauvinist culture (1994:90). As she aptly puts it, heterosexual black women "have traded the sexual restrictions of the patriarchy for casual sex, but their bodies have become casualties of sexuality dominated and defined by male desire" (90–91).

Finding healthy heterosexual ties has always been diffi-cult for black women. It is easy to understand the difficul-ties during slave times. Throughout our history, we have had to fight our public image. As Paulla Ebron (1991) makes clear, black women's negative public image does not always come from outside black culture. Ebron argues that popular images of black women are integral to sexist black male constructions of masculinity. She moves beyond most critics who present rap artists as either revolutionaries or purely misogynist ogres to suggest that men are using such images to speak to each other about masculinity.

Bell hooks's approach to studying black women is particularly helpful on issues surrounding sexuality. She is very much influenced by recent cultural studies approaches that foreground the study of images and spectatorship, and she has developed as a major concern of her work the image of black women in public culture, black female audience response, and black women as image producers. Examples of this project can be found in *Black Looks* (1992), *Outlaw Culture* (1994), and *Art on My Mind* (1995). From these books emerges a thoughtful—if, as I discuss later, somewhat heterosexist—treatment of the exploitation of black women's sexuality by public culture.

In "Eating and the Other: Desire and Resistance," from *Black Looks,* hooks moves far beyond merely identifying negative images of black women; she zeros in on the ways that racial and ethnic difference is used in films to obscure racial domination at the same time that it creates erotic desire. This erotic desire then leads people into a commodified culture. Hooks asks whether the increasing focus on race, Otherness, and difference can be pleasurable and a challenge to white supremacy. She cautions, "The over-riding fear is that cultural, ethnic, and racial differences will be continually modified and offered up as new dishes to enhance the white palate—that the Other will be eaten, consumed, and forgotten" (1992:39). Thus, hooks assumes commodification to be in and of itself bad rather than a form of social relations that *can* be exploitative.[4]

Hooks's work becomes more insightful when she speaks of the relationship between desire and resistance. Perhaps because black feminists have remained weary of the Eurocentrism in Freudian narratives, most have avoided speaking of desire and the unconscious. Hooks's writing has offered much-needed intervention in this area. For example, she shows the work of the unconscious and resistance: "Acknowledging ways the desire for pleasure, and that includes erotic longings, informs our politics, our understanding of difference, we may know better how desire disrupts, subverts, and makes resistance possible" (1992:39). Hooks does not cast viewers as merely passive recipients of negative images. Although most black women do passively absorb negative images, according to hooks, a few resist these images. These few critical black female spectators experience what she calls the pleasure of interrogation. Pleasure stems from constantly subjecting public images of African Americans to critical scrutiny. I, for one, certainly identify with hooks's description of the black feminist spectator who takes pleasure in figuring out the subtleties of racism in contemporary public culture. There is a seductive gratification to be found in constructing a resisting identity and transgressing the dominant ideology. I suggest that most black feminists experience such pleasure; it is what leads us to break with the overwhelmingly negative images of ourselves that surround our lives.

Hooks's critical black female spectator, however, appears to be exclusively heterosexual. Unfortunately, hooks misses every opportunity to interrogate the heterosexist biases in the dominant discourses on black female sexuality. She seems to assume that all black women identify with female characters, and she ignores the chance to see the emergence of a critical black lesbian spectator. For at least some lesbian spectators, the disruptions created by dis-ease with the assumed direction of female desire stimulate or heighten critical viewership.

Heterosexist bias runs throughout hooks's work. In her well-known essay on the film *Paris Is Burning* in *Black Looks* (1992), she finds no way to identify with the film's transvestites, because she does not see race as a structure of dominance that can be inflected by sexuality. To hooks, the film's producer and director, Jenny Livingston, is an outsider or voyeur, who must objectify her "subjects." In fact, Livingston identifies with the queens in her film in part because they are gay, as her brother was, but this connection was apparently unimportant to hooks. Further, we never see hooks interrogate her own discomfort at the disruption that black men who pose as women cause to dominant heterosexual culture.

In the *Black Looks* discussion of *Passion of Remembrance*, a film produced by the Afro-British collective Sankofa, hooks argues that a space has been created for black female subjectivity. She describes a scene in which two friends, Louise and Maggie, stand in front of a mirror as they dress for a party:

> Louise and Maggie claim the "gaze." Looking at one another, staring in mirrors, they appear completely focused on their encounter with black femaleness. How they see themselves is most important, not how they will be stared at by others. . . . They display their bodies not for voyeuristic colonizing gaze but for that look of recognition that affirms their subjectivity—that constitutes them as spectators. (1992:130)

Sounds erotic to me. Yet nowhere does hooks mention that Louise and Maggie are lovers. They "claim the 'gaze'" by asserting mutual sexual pleasure. Not only do they disrupt racist and sexist representations of female bodies; they call into question heterosexual assumptions as well. Lesbianism is key to the transgressive nature of this film.

In *Art on My Mind: Visual Politics*, hooks tells us that she has a lesbian sister she calls V. Since hooks's self-referential style includes many critical stories of her sisters, it is not surprising that she seems to have learned little about lesbianism from her. Instead, hooks describes V. in harsh terms:

> Always a daddy's girl. I was not surprised that my sister V. became a lesbian, or that her lovers were always white women. Her worship of Daddy and her passion for whiteness appeared to affirm a movement away from black womanhood and, of course, away from that image of the woman we did not want to become—our mother. (1995:34)

The relationship between V.'s lesbianism, her passion for whiteness, and her connection to her father remains unclear. In the context of a work that denies lesbian desire, however, it is hard for me to resist reading a subtext here that claims that lesbianism represents alienation from black womanhood.

Very little theory has been written on black lesbian desire. I suspect that, for some, the choice of lesbianism itself can alienate one from the race (compare Moraga 1983). After all, blackness is popularly assumed to be heterosexual. Most black lesbians have probably experienced the implicit assumption or explicit attack that we are traitors to the race. "The race" becomes a threatening place where self-hatred for sexual difference finds active community support.

Surely, there are many reasons black lesbians might be attracted to white women. Hooks's sister V. needs no excuses made for her. What is more important is to bring into focus a wider range of female desire than hooks's work allows. For hooks to take her work further, she will have to incorporate an understanding of heterosexism into her analysis.

I have to admit that hooks's narrow view of sexuality makes me angry. Her position does not take seriously the leadership roles of black lesbians such as Audre Lorde, Barbara Smith, and Cheryl Clarke in the formation of feminism. All of that work that we black lesbians have done to expose the relationship between sexism and heterosexism lies yet again unexplored by a sister.

As conservative black churches and some nationalists persist in condemning homosexuality as a threat to the very existence of the black community, black lesbians face even harsher accusations of disloyalty than do other black feminists. As long as lesbians can be isolated, all black women will suffer as accusations of lesbianism scare women away from our feminist ideas.

Although I have criticized hooks harshly for her heterosexism, I must emphasize that she has been the most influential voice among black feminists since Audre Lorde. Her books have been responsible for introducing many black women to the ideas of black feminism. In writing about black sexuality and the unconscious, among other areas, she has explored ideas that few have had the courage to engage. I greatly appreciate her work.

Conclusion

As I put the finishing touches on this chapter, I discovered that the Nation of Islam was preparing a second atonement march on Washington. Scheduled to take place just before the 2000 national election, the Million Family March attempted to build on the successes of the Million Man March of 1995. The Million Man March frightened many black feminists because we felt that it would herald a dramatic resurgence of black male sexism. A number of feminists who banded together to oppose the march, including Barbara Ramsby, Evelynn Hammonds, and Angela Davis, formed African American Agenda 2000 and made numerous useful interventions in the media. For example, the February 16, 1996, issue of *USA Today* quoted Kimberlé Crenshaw's emphasis of the narrowness of the march's agenda: "A unity that is purchased through the exclusion of the interests of specific obstacles facing 50% of the community is ill begotten unity." Fortunately—despite attempts to spread its ideology through local coordinating committees, through the 1997 Million Woman March in Philadelphia, and through the 1998 Million Youth March in New York— the Million Man March movement fell apart as a result of its own inaction, contradictory positions, and inappropriate exclusion of politically useful progressive black people.

The Million Family March seems like an attempt to revive the Nation of Islam after its leader, Minister Louis Farrakhan, disappeared from the media due to poor health and after the Nation of Islam's attempts to court white, rightwing support. Unfortunately, the basis for this march appeared to maintain many sexist and heterosexist biases. In a message accompanying the march's agenda, Farrakhan wanted to make it clear that, when he called for the march, he intended it for the traditional-looking family: "The human being has a need to be loved and that love is the nurturing force of the life in that human being. Therefore, every human being has the need for nurturing. Therefore, there is a need for a mother, a need for a father, and the need for family as the basic institution for the nurturing of the values that make us human beings." In placing the family at the center of a black agenda, Farrakhan builds on a long tradition of the racialized discourse of black nationalists and white racists. In most narratives about "The Problem" in the black community, failed family bonds figure prominently. Such statements have been made by not only Farrakhan but also, among others, Ron Karenga, Patrick Moynihan, and Bill Moyers; all agree that, to its detriment, the black community has weak family bonds in which a man is neither present nor head of the household. Thus, the building blocks for a strong community do not include welfare-dependent families; female-headed households; and especially gay, bisexual, and lesbian family members. This narrative does not find acceptable the families in which many of us live. Clearly, the Million Family March was not calling people together to support the heterogeneous families that make up black society; instead, the march supported a single model for black families, one with a male, a female, and children.

The prospect of yet another conservative, sexist, and heterosexist march in Washington reconfirmed for me the need for strong black feminist voices. I have discussed many of these voices in this chapter, and I have proposed an alternative narrative of their development. In addition, I have reviewed what many black feminist theorists have to say about family, class, and gender, in the hope that we will develop a dialogue about such topics that deepens our thinking.

I have explored the differences among black feminist theorists, because I believe that we need to look more critically at our own work to clarify our political positions. I have not forgotten, however, that virtually all black feminists share the same concern. Most centrally, black feminists are concerned by the negative impact that interactions between categories of identity, such as sexuality, race, class, and gender, have on black women's lives. Because of our shared interests, we have much room for dialogue.

Notes

1. Stephanie Shaw (1996) argues that during the Jim Crow era, this contradiction was resolved by the "socially responsible individualism" (2) of black professional women. Her book, which is less critical of middle-class black women than is Higginbotham's and my writing, gives a wonderful analysis of eighty black women's lives during Jim Crow. See also Linda Perkins 1983.

2. Combahee had not yet come to theorize sexuality, as some of its members—including Barbara Smith and Evelynn Hammonds—would do later. The group's understanding of the conflicts between straight and lesbian black women was just emerging.

3. Hooks's argument that white women did not labor in the fields grossly underestimates the number of poor farming families that either owned no slaves or worked alongside the few slaves that they did own. Here hooks perpetuates the romanticized vision of a South with many large plantations, lazy aristocrats, and numerous house servants. Unlike slaves in the Caribbean, most U.S. slaves worked on farms rather than on large plantations.

4. On this point, I am influenced by Paulla Ebron's 1999 essay "Tourists as Pilgrims."

2 The Dark Continent of Our Bodies

Constructing Science, Race, and Womanhood in the Nineteenth Century

We know less about the sexual life of little girls than of boys. But we need not feel ashamed of this distinction; after all, the sexual life of adult women is the "dark continent" for psychology.
—Freud, *The Question of Lay Analysis*

In the "scientific mind" no less than in the "popular imagination" of the nineteenth century, Africa represented an unknown and frightening place. It was a continent that needed exploring and controlling. So, too, was the psychology and biology of women. Through the privileged discourse of social evolution, these concerns came together. The acknowledged great thinkers, increasingly scientifically trained men, developed a discourse that simultaneously helped place women and people of color at the bottom of social hierarchies. Indeed, ideas about women and people of color were interdependent.

In this chapter I explore the ways nineteenth-century scientists used intertwined concepts of race and gender to build

81

a hegemonic worldview. My arguments depend on the view that race and gender are human inventions or social constructions that exaggerate minor differences among humans. Further, these social constructions are neither separate nor parallel concepts; rather, the concepts are constructed in relationship to each other. In other words, we cannot understand race without reference to gender, and we cannot understand gender without reference to race (see Spillers 1984).

On the surface, the relationship between race and gender may seem natural or forever linked in the same way. But it is possible to expose the construction of these human inventions, however unconscious this construction might have been. Kathleen Brown (1996), for example, demonstrates how early-modern Europeans used gender relations as an analogy to help them understand race. Because elite men of this era thought they understood gender relations, they created their knowledge and understanding of unfamiliar peoples of non-European backgrounds with reference to those social relations.

Today we debate whether it is appropriate to compare the situation of blacks to that of women or gays. When second-wave feminism emerged in the 1960s and 1970s, feminists used analogies between race and gender to clarify the "position of women." Many African Americans complained that such arguments demonstrated callous disregard for the impact of white racism on black lives. More recently, the debate over gays in the military included concerns about whether it was appropriate to turn to race to understand the exclusion and repression of gays and lesbians in the armed forces.

Our society is structured hierarchically by race; gender; sexuality; and, of course, class. Clearly, some analogies between these categories make sense. As Henry Louis Gates

(1999) shows, however, analogies can take us a long way in understanding prejudice, but they are not without limitations. He reminds us, for example, that both blacks and gays have been represented as sexually uncontrollable and predatory but that gay men and lesbians do not suffer transgenerational oppression as a category the way that blacks do. As Gates and others have also pointed out, analogies often suppress knowledge about the intersections of structures of dominance and lead to the invisibility of, for example, black women (see Wiegman 1995).

In this chapter, I argue that many of the analogies between race and gender make sense to us because of a specific history in which concepts of race and gender came to depend on each other. The rise of racial science in the nineteenth century began to set up a way of seeing social relations that assumed that race and gender had biological roots. (Sexuality did not emerge as a major focus until the end of the century.) Since both race and gender were biological realities and sex between genders was necessary to create race, the two categories seemed naturally linked in the nineteenth-century mind.

During the 1800s, scientists working in such emerging branches of fields as comparative anatomy, physiology, histology, and paleontology took the lead in explaining the naturalness of social relations. Many considered themselves progressive thinkers who wanted to use natural laws to reform society. In an effort to undermine what they considered to be outdated superstitions and religious beliefs, these progressives attempted to abstract and classify the flood of information about the world that the sciences were producing.

Indeed, many progressives engaged in a crusade against superstition or prescientific thinking. To help popularize science, these scientists set out to prove that superstition was a deviant practice followed only by primitive, childish, and lower-class people. Their writings appealed to a literate middle class, especially those with an upwardly mobile drive and a desire to be distinguished by acquiring high culture. Scientific knowledge increasingly became a part of this culture, and scientists stood out as models for those interested in exhibiting their access to that culture. As professionals concerned with diffusing and popularizing knowledge that was meant to explain the natural world objectively, their prestige as morally superior men grew. In turn, their prejudices gained hegemonic power and further influenced the development of science itself.

Although science did not create racism, it legitimated and helped solidify a new kind of racism for the industrial age. At the same time and in a dialectical fashion, racism contributed to the growth of science as a privileged worldview because scientists' beliefs were largely congruent with the dominant ideology (see Stepan 1993). The same can be said of the relationship between science and sexism. Clearly, asymmetrical gender relations and many of the ideologies that supported these relations preceded the rise of science as an authoritative voice on the subject of women. But science legitimated these views, and its own importance increased partly because it seemed to offer useful explanations about women's position in a changing and increasingly industrialized and colonized world.

Biology played a key role in the rise of science and the solidifying of racism and sexism, as biological models became paramount in explaining most social relations. As Sander Gilman has argued, "After Darwin the description of the biological world became what . . . the psychoanalytical model would be for the twentieth century—the source of universal explanation of causality through analogy" (1985b:70). As people sought to understand the world, they used biological models to move from the known (biology) to the unknown (social relations). They saw not only an analogy but also a causal connection between the two.

Playing the role of the central explanatory model, biology helped establish evolutionary theory as a seemingly value-free and unassailable view of the world. At the same time, evolutionary theory helped establish biology's position as the central explanatory model. As Martin Fichmann comments, "That it should have been evolutionary biology, literally the most human of sciences—and one with a great bearing on general culture—that contributed to the triumph of the concept of science as a value-neutral but inherently progressive enterprise . . . is a paradox worth exploring" (1984:471). Evolutionary biology was, in fact, far from a value-neutral and disinterested discipline; it depended on social prejudices to make itself understood. At the same time, it helped to firmly entrench these prejudices in the prevailing ideology of the day. Evolutionary theory both made sense of and justified the enormous expansion of Western power and the internal changes being wrought in gender relations.

Unlike most contemporary scientists, whose ideas tend to be expressed in a highly specialized vocabulary, the evolutionary theorists of the nineteenth century shared a common language with the literate people of their time. As Gillian Beer (1983) points out, this shared discourse allowed scientists to make use of familiar analogies, metaphors, and narrative patterns in communicating their ideas to nonscientists. Metaphors are essential to the scientific enterprise, as Sander Gilman (1985c) and Nancy Stepan (1993) have shown; in the sciences of human difference, especially, these metaphors can have normative repercussions. By bringing to these shared metaphors of inequality new, "scientific" methods and technologies, "the analogies became 'naturalized' in the language of sciences and their metaphorical nature was disguised" (Stepan 1993:363). In other words, these analogies and metaphors "revealed" the truths of nature and were, in turn, seen as the truth itself.

By the early twentieth century, Sigmund Freud's statement, that "the sexual life of adult women is the 'dark continent' for psychology" (1953:34–35), undoubtedly could be made with the confidence that (1) his readers shared the belief that too little was known about Africa and (2) his analogy—drawing as it does on images of the exotic, the frightening, and the primitive—would make sense to them. Ironically, the women he had in mind at the time were almost certainly white women—black women seem strangely absent from this reference to our homeland. Nonetheless, the images of black women—from Africa and its diaspora—played a formative role in the representation of European and Euro-American women whose psychology Freud went on to describe (see Brown 1996; Carby 1985; Stoler 1996).

This use of "the Other" to define the self took place during an era of heightened white supremacy at home and imperialism abroad. A number of nineteenth-century developments that we tend to think of as unrelated combined to produce a deluge of material on people of color. In the United States, the ruling classes imposed segregation on blacks in the South, on Chicanos in the Southwest, and on Asians in the West. In addition, the state completed its project of forcing Native Americans onto segregated reservations. At the same time, the United States was expanding its power into Mexico, the Caribbean, and the Pacific.[1] And the country was participating in a broader international phenomenon, as the West came to dominate 80 percent of the world's people by the end of the century (see Said 1978).

As Edward Said points out in *Orientalism* (1978), the nineteenth century witnessed a flood of written material and an explosion of discourses on race and people of color. Said notes that these expanding discourses paralleled and assisted imperialism. His analyses and much of the work that has been influenced by his thinking help explain the intensity with which nineteenth-century scholars worked to construct a worldview that justified and interpreted the enormous expansion of Western power and the internal changes in political economy and gender relations. Of course, these scholars did not all agree on how the world should be understood. Some defended the working classes against the bosses, others supported feminist movements, and some even exhibited anti-imperialist sentiments. But a surprising number fell prey to racist evolutionary beliefs. And they often turned to these beliefs about race, by way of analogy, to understand the rest of the world.

By the late eighteenth century, with the early stages of exploration and imperialism having created the conditions for it, a racist science of human differences had already been well established. Over the course of the nineteenth century, scientists also turned their attention to gender, expanding their concerns beyond women's reproductive difference from men. To understand gender differences, they depended on their system for understanding race. In a complicated use of metaphors, racial difference could be used to explain gender difference and vice versa. Stepan explains:

Once "woman" had been shown to be indeed analogous to lower races by the new science of anthropometry and had become, in essence, a racialized category, the traits and qualities special to woman could be in turn used in an analogical understanding of lower races. These analogies now had the weight of empirical reality and scientific theory. The similarities between a Negro and a white woman, or between a criminal and a Negro, were realities of nature, somehow "in" the individuals studied. (1993:614)

Again, we see this analogy at work in Freud's remark about the sexual life of adult women. His readers could understand what he had to say about white women because he compared them to the so-called savages of Africa. Women are the savages of Western civilization, and savages are the women of the human race. Seemingly obvious inferiority was thus used to explain less-apparent inferiority. These analogies also worked because they were allied with a common system of beliefs. Stepan points out that ideas and anxieties about disease, sexual behavior, and moral development were all expressed in terms of race, gender, and class—the central human differences of the nineteenth century.

To understand how these interdependent ideas of race and gender worked in practice, it is useful to take a closer look at primary sources. Particularly useful are Darwin's *The Descent of Man* ([1871] n.d.) and *Popular Science Monthly* (1872–1999), the latter being one of the journals that helped spread Darwinism in the United States. I have chosen these two sources because, as John C. Burnham (1982) suggests, they played central roles in disseminating scientific ideas about human differences throughout the educated classes.

The Uncivilized Darwin

I, probably along with most people who had not studied the history of science, once believed that Charles Darwin was a "pure" scientist who was unencumbered by social prejudice. I thought it was social Darwinists, such as Herbert Spencer, who were the true racists and sexists and who had distorted Darwin's theories. This implication is found in works as diverse as Johannes Fabian's *Time and the Other* (1983) and Dale Spender's *Women of Ideas and What Men Have Done to Them* (1983). But upon reading Darwin's work itself, I discovered that it took very little to distort his thinking into social Darwinism or even into the more conservative elements of today's sociobiology. It is unclear to me why Darwin's more racist and sexist ideas have gone largely unnoticed. His antislavery positions are often highlighted, but antislavery attitudes do not necessarily reflect antiracist thinking. Perhaps it is difficult to acknowledge the roles of racism and sexism in the success of a major scientific figure such as Darwin. We have limited tools of analysis that force us to dismiss everything about someone we find to be racist or sexist. As a consequence, we limit our understanding by ignoring the complexities of our history.

The recognition of Darwin's own prejudices need not deflect attention from his impressive achievements. The radical implications of his work in developing evolutionary theory remain part of the intellectual heritage of philosophical materialism that I claim as my own. Stephen Jay Gould (1981) tells us that the ultimate nineteenth-century materialist, Karl Marx, recognized these radical implications. Writing to Friedrich Engels, Marx alerted his colleague to the fact that *The Origin of the Species* ([1859] n.d.) contained the basis in natural history for their views.

Astute readers, such as Marx, had to infer for themselves the larger implications of the argument in *Origin of the Species.* As early as 1838, Darwin noted in his journal that he believed the human mind was simply brain matter on which divine intervention had no direct impact (see Gould 1981). Yet in his first book, he chose to leave unarticulated his evolutionary theory's implications for humans, stating simply that, in the future, "light will be thrown on the origin of man and his history" ([1859] n.d.:373). It was not until 1871 that Darwin explicitly presented his heretical views, in *The Descent of Man and Selection in Relation to Sex.*

In this book, Darwin asked three interrelated questions: "firstly, whether man, like every other species, is descended from some pre-existing form; secondly, the manner of his development; and thirdly, the value of the differences between the so-called races of men" ([1871] n.d.:390). Darwin's answers to these questions were particularly important because he was speaking into hotly contested contemporary debates on race and gender. With *The Descent of Man,* he was entering into these controversies with the authority of a well-established scientist who would dispassionately explain some of the central mysteries of human life. Indeed, Darwin ended up playing a key role in fixing the boundaries of race and gender, even as he disrupted the definitions of a species. He believed that the only way to decide whether humans had descended from some preexisting form—that is, apes— was to ask whether "man" "varies himself and whether his variation is transmitted to his offspring by the laws that animals use" (395). Thus, much of *The Descent of Man* was directed at proving that all races of "mankind" are of the same species. Although Darwin took the radical stance that science proves we are all one species, albeit a mutable one, he relied on perceived differences among humans to prove his evolutionary thesis.

Darwin focused on both the similarities and the differences among humans in establishing the contours of race, gender, and species. In terms of similarities, he examined the human mind and concluded that "the lowest savage shares more in kind with the civilized man than the most highly organized ape" ([1871] n.d.:445). One of his major sources for this conclusion was his own experience on a voyage to South America. As many have pointed out, his evolutionary theory crystallized through observations of the animals and plants of that region. But his study of the Fuegians from the tip of South America also influenced his thinking. Darwin's observations of three Fuegian "specimens" taken on board his vessel, the *Beagle*, led him to conclude that they had the power to reason the way "civilized" people do. But he also uncovered certain differences, which led him to agree with Herbert Spencer—whom he called "our great philosopher" (Darwin [1871] n.d.:492)—that savages are more likely to imitate behavior than are civilized men (451).

Central to Darwin's argument that we are all one species was his discussion of whether or not the various races could produce offspring. He easily proved that interracial sex produces progeny, noting that "the races of man are not sufficiently distinct to inhabit the same country without fusion; and the absence of fusion affords the usual and best test of specific distinctness" ([1871] n.d.:636). In Darwin's use of the word "fusion," we have one of the best examples of scientific discourse stripping the real meaning from human action. Many other commentators of his day referred to fusion as miscegenation. With the work of Angela Davis (1981) and other black feminists, we know that a simpler term is more precise: "rape." In general, Darwin's detached review of the ethnographic literature on peoples of color carefully obscures the realities of conquest, pillage, and rape. According to accounts such as Darwin's, the races in the places in question were simply in a process of "fusion"—a word that calls no attention to the reality of forceful domination that was at work.

Darwin turned to the United States to explore this question of fusion further, attempting to explain what appeared to be the small number of mulattos in the United States "considering the circumstances" ([1871] n.d.:533). (Of course, "considering the circumstances" glosses white men's freedom to rape—or fuse with?—black women.) He suggested that the seemingly low fertility rate of mulattos resulted from the degraded and anomalous position of their class; their absorption into the black race; and, of course, the assumed profligacy of mulatto women (533). Here again, the analogy between gender and race was alive and well.

Darwin was particularly concerned to explain why people of color seemed to die out when confronted with Western civilization: "When civilized nations come into contact with barbarians the struggle is short, except where a deadly climate gives its aid to the native race" ([1871] n.d.:543). He noted the impact of disease and warfare on natives, but his primary concern was to explain why colonized peoples appeared to be less fertile. Having proven interfertility between races, Darwin suggested that savages became more sterile when they met civilized people, because they were being exposed to new conditions. Civilized peoples, like domesticated animals, he reasoned, were accustomed to more varying conditions (549). Here savages were seen as primitive, simple human beings, whereas civilized people were seen as more complex and cultured. It was the complexity of civilized humans that allowed them to survive interracial contact.

To further explain differences between races and to obscure the impact of imperialism, Darwin used gender as an explanatory tool. Here the position of women was used to explain the deficiencies of a race: "The chief causes [of racial inferiority] are, first, so-called communal marriages or promiscuous intercourse; secondly, the consequences of female infanticide; thirdly, early betrothals; and lastly, the low estimation in which women are held as mere slaves" ([1871] n.d.:893). Europeans could relax: Conquest had little to do with degeneracy; underdeveloped biology and primitive gender relations were at fault.

Having proven that the races are all one species (racial differences notwithstanding), Darwin turned to explaining how different men are from women. Across the races, men were seen as "more courageous, pugnacious and energetic than women and [had] a more inventive genius" ([1871] n.d.:867). Women, for their part, were seen as being more tender and less selfish. Darwin was convinced that, even in lower savages, man was superior to woman. Here the analogy between gender and race depended on a system of thought that viewed all savages and all women as somehow inferior to white men.

Darwin was taking part in that era's bourgeois Western obsession with the gender relations among non-Western peoples. Travelers and armchair anthropologists alike were preoccupied with debating the natural roles for women by using evidence collected from around the world. As Rosalind Coward shows in *Patriarchal Precedents* (1983), nineteenth-century scholars assumed that gender relations were the most basic human social relationships and that the way to begin to understand this dimension and others in more complex societies was by looking to simpler times or less-complex cultures. These discussions had the double effect of contributing to the debates on the "woman question" and on race relations. On one hand, these scholars used their understanding of women's status in primitive societies to determine what the roles should be for women in the West. On the other hand, they used their understanding of what women's status should be to determine the level of civilization of non-Western peoples.

As Darwin looked around the world, he came to adopt a rather conservative position on women in the West. He argued that it was possible to change some of women's inferior characteristics but only with great effort. Here Darwin was speaking directly to the era's controversy over educating women. He helped undermine women's efforts to obtain education by suggesting that, because little girls had not yet reached puberty, early schooling did little to develop their potential. To affect evolution, girls would have to be vigorously trained near adulthood; then these women would have to be selected for marriage more frequently than other women. But since men "generally undergo a severe struggle in order to maintain themselves and their families ... this [would] tend to keep up or even increase their mental powers, and, as a consequence, the present inequality between the sexes" would persist ([1871] n.d.:874–75). Alas, women were destined to remain inferior.

Darwin's review of the ethnographic literature led him to conclude that sexual inequality was more pronounced among civilized people than among savages. (He approvingly noted the speculation of German anatomist Carl Vogt that the differences between the cranial cavity of the sexes increases with the development of a race so that the European male excels the European female much more than the "negro the negress" [(1871) n.d.:876 n. 26].) Similarly for Darwin, the greater the inequality between the sexes, the more civilized a race was.

In addition to believing that sexual inequality was more pronounced among the civilized than among the savage, Darwin believed that sexual selection contributed to the differences among the races. Oddly enough—at least to those of us who are used to a different standard of scientific objectivity—Darwin turned to standards of beauty to prove this point. His argument rested on the premise that, in the human species, males fight each other for control of females. Thus, through sexual selection, strength is passed on to the heirs of the victors of these fights. At the same time, men choose as mates those women who meet their race's standards of beauty. The attributes that appeal to men are slowly and gradually exaggerated, "having selected during many generations for their wives the most strongly characterized and therefore most attractive women" ([1871] n.d.:908). Since these standards vary from race to race, different characteristics are bred into each race over time. "For my own part," Darwin revealed, "I conclude that of all the causes which have led to the differences in external appearance between the races of man, and to a certain extent men and the lower animals, sexual selection has been the most efficient" (908). From this—believing apparently in the "objective" validity of his own standards—Darwin concluded that there was a link between the perceived ugliness of primitive peoples and their inferiority.

Ludmilla Jordanova's book on the images of women in science and medicine helps explain the atmosphere in which Darwin turned to beauty to make his point:

In general, there was a strong aesthetic component in medical writings on women in this period. Discussing the
beauty of the breast in the same breath as its vital nutritive
function indicates how tightly linked and highly charged
medical and social values were. The breast was good,
morally and biologically, hence its attractiveness and the
resultant sociability between the sexes. The social and natural domains were brought together here; furthermore,
medical thinking depended on a rich set of images and
metaphors that appealed not only to the imagination but
specifically to visual pleasure. (1989:30)

It is not surprising, then, that when Darwin turned his
aesthetic gaze on nonwhite women, he produced some of
his most offensive observations. At one point, he quoted Sir
Andrew Smith, who "once saw a (Hottentot) woman who
was considered a beauty, and she was so immensely developed behind, that when seated on level ground she could
not rise, and had to push herself along until she came to a
slope" (quoted in Darwin [1871] n.d.:885). By quoting
Smith, Darwin was writing into a spirited debate about "the
missing link" between human and ape. There had been
much speculation that the Hottentot were the link between
human and animal. More appropriately called the Khoikhoi
or Quena today, the so-called Hottentot live in southern
Africa, a region the British were struggling with mixed success to control during the late nineteenth century. Many
Europeans viewed them as the most savage of all people,
and the West became obsessed with both their buttocks and
the shape of their women's labia (see Gilman 1985a).

Undoubtedly Darwin and many of his contemporary readers knew about Saartjie Baartman, popularly known as the
Hottentot Venus. In 1810 she arrived in England on a five-

year contract to work as a maid and to be exhibited in carnival-like conditions. She was a sensation, first in England and then in France. During her five-year stay in Europe, she became celebrated in both popular culture and scientific discourse. She was the subject of popular songs, vaudeville acts, and cartoons. At the same time, Georges Cuvier, a well-known naturalist, described her in detail after examining her first while she was alive and again during a famous autopsy. Although he wrote in a somber scientific tone, his texts now sound as funny in places as some of the popular verses.

In contrast, Darwin used humor purposely, not to undermine his argument but to draw his readers into his line of reasoning. He also alluded to both the scientific and the popular narratives of the Hottentot Venus in his use of the example of the Khoikhoi woman who supposedly could not stand on her own. Ironically, Darwin's humorous tone fits like a missing link between popular and scientific discourses on race and gender. When it comes to African women, they deserve only humor in his narrative.

For the preeminent scientist of the nineteenth century, discussions about race and gender were inseparable. Darwin saw quite clearly the implications of his early work for Western society, and he drew them out explicitly for those who might not understand his studies of plants and animals. He used analogies based on race and gender to create a science of human culture. His use of a disinterested scientist's tone combined with a confidence that allowed him to make occasional excursions into humor was rhetorically persuasive. He was far from being the distanced, objective scientist that his tone might have suggested, and he was in a privileged position to influence the debates of his day. Indeed, his work was widely read precisely *because* he so effectively defended bourgeois white male power—a power based on the simultaneous control of people of color, white women, and the working classes. Darwin's work took on the issues that emanated from this control with arguments that naturalized the harsh realities of social oppression.

Darwin Diffused into the Popular Imagination

The pre-eminence of the female sex over the male, occurring only in certain inferior species and races, and in children of the superior races, marks an inferior degree of evolution. The same may be said of equality of the sexes, which is observable only among individuals little advanced in evolution: inferior races and species, youth, aged persons, and the lower classes. On the contrary, the pre-eminence of the male over the female represents a superior phase of evolution, for it characterizes superior species and races, the adult age, and the higher classes. In the moral as in the physical point of view, evolution appears to me, then, to advance from the pre-eminence of the female sex to that of the male sex; equality of the sexes would thus be a stage in the natural transition between two opposite phases of evolution.

—G. Delauney (1881:192)

In this quote from *Popular Science Monthly*, Delauney[2] uses evolutionary theory to justify his era's major social prejudices concerning gender, race, age, and class. Each social prejudice is used as an analogy to explain the others. An accompanying editorial defends the editor's decision to publish the Delauney article despite fears of backlash from readers. The editor notes sarcastically that he expects attacks for his service to science: "Our own special trouble is, that in about six weeks we shall get a bushel, more or less, of answers to [Delauney's piece], written very much alike, all in 'hair-marks,' and with very pale ink" (Youmans 1881:275). Bolstered by scientific theory, however, the editor assures his readers that he will not succumb to a feminist backlash. Interestingly, he does not seem to expect as much as a response from the so-called inferior races or the lower classes.

The founding editor of *Popular Science Monthly*, Edward Livingston Youmans, often used evolutionary theories to argue against middle-class women's demands for the vote and for higher education. In so arguing, he ignored a central irony in his own life. During his early adult years, temporary blindness impeded his work. Fortunately, his sister, Eliza Youmans, a science educator in her own right, carried out his experiments for him until he regained his eyesight (see Fiske 1894).

Youmans justified his attacks on feminism by what he considered the greatest contribution to civilization's progress, the spread of scientific knowledge. Indeed, the far-reaching spread of Darwinian ideas and scientific knowledge generally owed much to the growth of magazines such as *Popular Science Monthly*. Beginning in the mid-nineteenth century, new magazines helped to fuel—and in turn benefited from—the growing fascination with science among the literate bourgeoisie. New technological advances captured their imaginations, and new journals—such as *Scientific American*, first published in 1845—were dedicated to spreading information about these inventions. The educated public was equally fascinated by debates about evolution. Inaugurated in 1872 to disseminate Herbert Spencer's theories in the United States, *Popular Science Monthly* led the way in capturing the demand for knowledge about general science.

Youmans identified his intended audience as the "generally-educated classes" of men who could use the journal for self-instruction in science. He suspected that educated men would be attracted to his journal because they would recognize the important role that science played in bringing humanity out of the thralldom of ignorance:

> Rightly to appreciate what science has accomplished for humanity, we must remember not only that it has raised men to the understanding and enjoyment of the beautiful order of Nature, but that it has put an end to the baneful superstitions by which, for ages, men's lives were darkened, to the sufferings of witchcraft, and the terrors of the untaught imagination which filled the world with malignant agencies. (Youmans 1872:114)

Indeed, Youmans saw the diffusion of science as the "next great task of civilization" (114). He wanted to play a prominent role in these developments, influencing school curricula and publishing a journal to spread the word. Not surprisingly some conservative, leading men accused Youmans of contributing to the degeneration of civilization rather than its progress. He was attacked in the pages of the stately *Scribner's Monthly,* and a number of religious leaders warned their followers not to read his blasphemous journal. At one point he wrote apprehensively to Spencer, his friend and main contributor, "The religious press is beginning to threaten us" (quoted in Fiske 1894:303).

Threats, however, apparently motivated Youmans more than they intimidated him; his campaign often had the flavor of a religious crusade, even as he attacked religion. As a leading crusader for science and against superstition, Youmans struggled to "naturalize" and define the liberal, progressive position, to make it appear unassailable because it was based on proven laws of nature. He pointed out the fallacies of religious arguments, even as, ironically, he unconsciously adapted the style of these arguments. He attacked conservatives opposed to reform movements that were influenced by scientific developments. Using the pages of *Popular Science Monthly* to influence public policy, he entered debates on education, the woman question, race relations, and class conflict. His success was reflected in impressive circulation figures: 11,000 by 1874 (see Mott 1938); this circulation made his magazine the most influential science journal of the nineteenth century.

The articles published by Youmans on the woman question, race relations, and other social dilemmas did not all share the same position. The range of positions on the woman question, for example, included both profeminist and antifeminist advocates. Similarly, some authors worried that African Americans were a threat to white people, whereas others suggested that they were no threat at all. What all the articles shared was reliance on scientific arguments to make their points. Despite these apparent differences in opinion, however, the overall impact of the journal was to support restrictions on the lives of women, people of color, and the working classes; the editorial hand of Youmans made certain of that. Profeminist articles were often followed by editorials undermining the author's authority. Similarly, an article by the intellectual black nationalist Edward Blyden (1878), which attacked Spencer for relying on inaccurate travelers' accounts, was published as a humorous curiosity. Youmans seemed to think it amusing that a black man would dare dispute the scientific writings of the editor's admired and erudite friend.

Many of the writers in *Popular Science Monthly* assumed a distanced, scholarly tone, much as Darwin did in most of his writings. These scientists sought to persuade by assuming the unassailable posture of methodical and systematic thinkers. But a number of articles and editorials adopted a more hysterical tone, especially when the authors perceived threats to "civilization." African Americans, feminists, and unruly workers often caused writers to lose their scholarly equilibrium. Writers also frequently used ridicule and sarcasm to argue against those who opposed any aspect of bourgeois white male control. Arguments for the rights of any oppressed people were often undermined by responses that purported to show the ridiculously unscientific manner in which they were argued. The authors often seemed amused that Africans or women would dare to think themselves equal to white men. To James B. Craighead, for example, it was absurd for blacks to imagine that better access to education would make them equal to whites:

> The freeman imagined that whatever superiority white people have over blacks is owing to education; and as Eve was induced to think that if she and Adam should eat of the forbidden fruit they would be as gods, so the ordinary African thought if his child could only read, write and cipher, he would be in every way the equal of the Caucasian. (Craighead 1884:41)

What a stupid woman Eve was! How equally stupid were black people for thinking that literacy would bring equality! Craighead asserted, "Scientists and the world admit the natural superiority of white races over the colored" (45). Similarly, numerous authors ridiculed women for demanding higher education and the vote. Ridicule, however, was not the sole intent of these arguments; the occasional hysterical warnings against degeneration revealed the serious aim behind the sarcastic tactics. As in Darwin's *Descent of Man*, the tone was more than an incidental element; rather, it was part of a strategy of persuasion.

As the preceding section on Darwin suggests, evolution-ary biologists and ethnologists took a leading role in responding to feminist agitation in the late nineteenth cen-tury; perceptions about gender relations in primitive soci-eties were used as models for arguing both for and against feminist positions. The evidence for these arguments came from travelers' accounts, many of which were published in *Popular Science Monthly.*

Taken separately, these accounts appeared merely to inform readers of curious practices, lifestyles, or even cloth-ing. Take, for example, W. B. Palgrave's report on Malays in the Philippines:

> But while the men's attire, though national in the main,
> shows occasional token of European influence, the women,
> with wise conservatism, retain their graceful Malay costume
> unaltered as of old. Wrapped in the many-colored folds of
> the silken *saya,* or *sarong,* and over it a second but narrower
> waist-cloth, also of silk, reaching down to the knees, and
> dark in hue; her breast and shoulders covered with delicate
> *pina* texture, while the matchless abundance of her raven
> hair ripples from under a white hooded kerchief far down
> her back not seldom to her very heels, a Malay woman
> could hardly even did she wish it, improve on the toilet
> bequeathed by her ancestors. (Palgrave 1878:454)

Such descriptions are not simply intended to be entertaining or informative, however. This one, with its erotic under-tones, depends on a notion of all women as naturally con-servative, preserving the ways of their culture. The Malay men exhibit a more adventurous spirit, imitating European ways to their detriment. Ann Laura Stoler has labeled the erotic undertones found in this quote "scientific pornogra-phy." She speaks of a pornographic racial taxonomy in which "the sexual pleasures of scientific knowledge join with the pornographic aesthetics of race" (1996:184).

Many travelers provided accounts in which women were presented as beasts of burden who were considered inferior in their own cultures. In 1882, Lieutenant G. Kreitler of Count Szechenyi's Central Asian Expedition reported on a "curious Burmese tribe":

> All the hard work among the Kacheen is done by the women and girls, who are up in the morning at their household duties while the men are still in bed.
>
> The woman does not venture to raise her eyes when she speaks with her husband or her employer. . . . The women are all the time at work, cutting roads through the thickets, driving the cattle to pasture, cleaning the house, getting the meals, and weaving cloth. The men perform no manual labor, or, at most, will once in a while go out into the field and show the women in a rough way how the tillage ought to be done. Their principal business is to smoke opium. Marriages among the lower classes are mere business affairs, in which the dowry and physical strength of the bride are the first considerations. (Kreitler 1882:329)[3]

Although many of the travelers reported on the inferior status of women, some accounts pointed to women's equal or superior place in their communities. The missionary Rev. W. G. Lawes, who spent three years in New Guinea for the London Missionary Society, reported to the Royal Geographical Society of London that the "burden of labor is fairly divided between 'New Guinea' men and women" (Lawes 1882:331).

It would seem that *Popular Science Monthly* readers might have considered the evidence given by Lawes and Kreitler to be contradictory, given the generally held belief that peoples considered to be living at the same primitive stage of civilization would have similar social relations. However, ethnologists and protosocial scientists massaged such contradictory observations into various theoretical positions. These writers, who were given prominent space in *Popular Science Monthly,* turned ethnographic curiosities into the building blocks of ideological positions. Their task was clear: Smooth over the contradictions between travelers' reports to explain, criticize, or justify gender relations at home. Luke Owen Pile, fellow of the Anthropological Society of London, performed this task well (Pile 1872). He relied on a variety of contradictory ethnographic reports to support the argument that certain rights, such as the vote, should not be extended to women. He reasoned that the call for women's suffrage ignored the realities of women as they have evolved over the centuries: "The woman for whom a vote is demanded is not, when carefully inspected, a woman of flesh and blood, but an abstract or archetypal idea for which the realists of the nineteenth century claim a positive existence" (88).

One can hear echoes of Darwin in many of the articles on the woman question. For example Ely Van de Warker, a gynecologist, argued that the fact that women of savage races "are in base servitude to the other sex is in obedience to the aggressive and belligerent character of all males of higher order animals. This has the force of law. . . . With the slow advent of civilization the differences between the sexes increase" (Van de Warker 1875:455).

Such arguments were, at times, challenged. In a feminist rejoinder to Van de Warker, Dr. Frances Emily White responded in the next issue:

Although the characteristics peculiar to each sex have undoubtedly been acquired under the operation of the same laws it would seem that men and women have become too much differentiated in their mode of living, for the physical or mental health of either. Among lower animals in a wild state, sex makes little difference in the habits of life; and, among barbarous tribes and races of men, there is little concerted action or differentiation of duties of men and women . . . ; and it has always been considered a sign of higher civilization when woman is released from the heavier kinds of labor, and relegated to a special and different sphere of activity. But civilization, even, may be carried too far. (F. E. White 1875:300)

Clearly, White was adding her voice to the bourgeois feminist movement that protested middle-class white women's restriction to a domestic sphere. As a highly educated woman, she must have felt this form of gender segregation very personally. But even White, like the gynecologist she disputed, resorted to racist arguments to defend her position on the woman question at home.

Although *Popular Science Monthly* included such profeminist arguments as the one by White, the editor often showed his hostility toward women's equality. Seldom did a profeminist article pass without negative comment from the Editor's Table. For example, Youmans published Dr. Emily Blackwell's defense of women's right to work, an article that showed how the domestic labor of "savage" women had been transformed into the labor performed by "civilized" men. Her argument suggested that women should be able to enter the factories, since the work performed there was once performed at home:

In the savage state, women built the wigwam, raised the corn, prepared the clothes, carried on in its rudest and most elementary form all the work which is today the object of modern industry. But since these simple forms of labor have devolved into architecture and agriculture and manufactures, it is held that women can not follow their old occupations under their new forms, under penalty of personal deterioration and social disaster. It is the conditions under which work is done, apparently, which constitute it domestic work, rather than the nature of the work itself. Weaving was domestic work when done at home, and ceased to be so when done in a factory. (Blackwell 1883:390)

Blackwell worried that the separation of the labor and domestic spheres would impede the object of advancing civilization, namely the development "of men and women into easy natural companionship" (396).

This argument had to both be taken seriously and contained, which Youmans tried to do in a piece from his Editor's Table, entitled "Progress and the Home." He began by reminding readers of an earlier editorial in response to an article by Dr. Dix on the woman question. Youmans had defended the Dix attack on providing higher education to women by suggesting that Dix's arguments were soundly based on the laws of nature and clearly demonstrated that different roles for men and women had evolved to form civilization. In defending Dix against feminist critics, he warned that "if there is one thing that pervades and characterizes what is called the 'woman's movement' it is the spirit of revolt against the home, and the determination to escape from it into the center sphere of activity that will bring her into direct and open competition with men" (Youmans 1883:412). Apparently, Youmans printed the Blackwell article as a dangerous example of feminist thinking rather than as a valuable contribution to scientific advancement.

Indeed, Youmans attacked Blackwell by drawing on anthropology, which he argued revealed an ancient, primordial sexual division of labor that was a fundamental condition to all social development. "Before industries began to take any separate shape," he argued, "there was already a division of occupations so broad and clear as to be evidently grounded in the nature of things, and all the subsequent progress of mankind has been achieved in subordination to it" (1883:413).

According to Youmans, Blackwell's position endangered the bonds of protection for women that could be found in both the predatory life of the savage and the civilized life of Western peoples. The family had evolved as an institution in which women's noncompetitive role was essential. In a hysterical tone, he warned:

> The precipitation of woman into the outer world of conflicts, where the strongest have their way, would involve a dissolution of human society, and is not even possible as an experiment. Granting that the protection of woman has always been, and is still, very imperfect, progress must consist in making it more perfect, and not in subverting the order of which it is a natural and necessary part.
> (1883:414)

In such arguments, the very progress of civilization seemed to be at stake. Despite their disagreement over the status of women, both Youmans and Blackwell assumed that nonwhite races were inferior. They used both the supposed differences and the similarities in gender relations among "superior" and "inferior" races to defend their version of civilized social relations. The similarities between races suggested to Youmans that sexual differences were so deeply embedded and natural that basic social relations would fall apart if people tampered with them. For her part, Blackwell argued that in ancient and savage societies women had always worked and therefore should continue to do so.

At the same time, differences between the ways societies constructed gender relations were viewed as signs of what separated the races. Any foolhardy tampering with these racial differences would plunge civilized nations into a degenerate, savage state. Both feminists and antifeminists assumed that differences in gender were reliable indicators of racial differences.

In another article, Grant Allen argued that even lowly savages "discriminate between pretty squaws or gins and plain ones, between handsome men and ugly ones" (Allen 1881:344). He followed Darwin's lead in showing the differences and similarities between races by highlighting the evolution of an aesthetic sense in humans. He claimed that civilized humans were distinguished by a more highly developed aesthetic faculty that included women's increasing use of the most beautiful costumes and ornaments. Similarly, Spencer, whose work was often featured in *Popular Science Monthly,* used the differing position of women to mark the distinctions between inferior and superior races. In a reprint published as "The Status of Women and Children," he wrote:

> Perhaps in no way is the moral progress of mankind more clearly shown than by contrasting the position of women among savages with their position among the most advanced of the civilized: at the one extreme a treatment of them cruel to the utmost degree bearable; at the other extreme a treatment which, in certain direction, gives them precedence over men. (Spencer 1876:433)

Spencer continued by detailing the distinctions between the sexes at the various stages of society's development. He wanted to expose the connection between the status of women and the type of social organization. As Darwin had done before him, he presented his arguments as a disinterested man of science who organized the facts collected by Western travelers in various parts of the world. He wrote with the kind of authority that left room for no dispute from reasonable men.

By contrast, the most hysterical-sounding articles on race that *Popular Science Monthly* published touched on race relations in the United States. In 1883, Youmans prominently featured E. W. Gilliam's antiblack piece, "The African in the United States." Like other writers, Gilliam relied on an understanding of sexual difference among superior peoples to explain differences between blacks and whites. He was also interested in elucidating the differences between classes:

> The laboring class (including blacks) is naturally the more fruitful class. In the case of a laboring woman the child-bearing is greater by a number of years than in one more delicately reared. Again, in estimating fecundity, the pain and danger attendant upon parturition are factors, and its comparative ease to the laboring woman, contrasted with the profound and long-continued prostration it brings to the lady of tender palms and jeweled fingers, is well known. (436–37)

Gilliam showed surprising faith in the white working class but warned that the advancing black race would menace all whites. He based his argument on the "natural law" that "the poor, lower, laboring class [will] naturally rise, while the rich upper class [will] descend" (1883:440). In this intertwined relationship between race and class, all the blacks are poor, and all the rich are white. He warned that natural law portends disaster: "No two free races, remaining distinctly apart, can advance side by side, without a struggle for supremacy. The thing is impossible. The world has never witnessed it, and *a priori* grounds are against it" (440). Like many other contributors to *Popular Science Monthly,* Gilliam was concerned about "miscegenation" between the two races. However, he concluded that large-scale miscegenation was unlikely to occur because social inequality between the races represented an insurmountable barrier.

Popular Science Monthly presented a range of opinions on miscegenation, including one that attacked the Supreme Court decision prohibiting interracial marriage (Lewis 1883). Also on this side of the debate stood the distinguished anthropologist M. A. de Quatrefages, whose article appeared in the first volume of the journal. De Quatrefages spoke out against polygenists, those who believed that the races were separate species. Later, in an abridged version of a *Revue Scientifique* article, "The Crossing of the Human Races," de Quatrefages argued:

> It is true that mongrels, born and grown up in the midst of
> the hatred of the inferior race and the contempt of the
> superior race, are liable to merit the reproaches which are
> commonly attached to them. On the other hand, if real
> marriages take place between the races, and their offspring
> are placed upon a footing of equality with the mass of the
> population, they are quite able to reach the general level,
> and sometimes to display superior qualities. (1880:167)

De Quatrefages had to be taken seriously; after all, he was an eminent French scientist. Nonetheless, such reasoning seemed to get lost in the barrage of racist arguments against miscegenation.

The belief that sexual appetites differed between whites and other races contributed to making miscegenation such a burning issue. Often this difference in morality was said to be based on climate. *Popular Science Monthly* could be seen pressing science into the service of advancing moral philosophy and exposing the different moral standards around the world. One article, for example, reported:

> Modern French scientists are nothing if not methodical, and have repeatedly called attention to the curious regularity in the geographical distribution of certain vices and virtues: intemperance, for instance, north of the forty-eighth parallel; sexual aberrations south of the forty-fifth; financial extravagance in large seaport towns; thrift in pastoral highland regions. (*Popular Science Monthly* 1888:37)

Of course, it was common to assume a lack of sexual morality among savage peoples.

As should be clear from the *Popular Science Monthly* articles quoted herein, it is often difficult to separate arguments about race that depend on assumptions about sexual difference from arguments about gender that depend on notions of race. It is as if the analogies became so intertwined that they began to collapse on each other. Nancy Stepan (1993) speaks of these intertwined analogies as a metaphorical system. For her, such a system "provided the 'lenses' through which people experienced and 'saw' the differences between classes, races, and sexes, between civilized man and the savage, between rich and poor, between the child and the adult" (362). This metaphorical system can be seen at work in Spencer's "Comparative Psychology of Man," as the author explained the inferiority of both women and savages. He argued that "limitation of heredity by sex may account both for those sexual differences of mind which distinguished men and women in all races and for those which distinguished them in each race, or each society" (1876:264–65). The civilized are considered superior in part because they are seen as having a greater mental modifiability than the uncivilized. Similarly, men are distinguished from women by their greater mental plasticity. Spencer continued:

> Along with comparisons of races in respect to mental plasticity may go parallel comparisons of the sexes in each race. Is it true always, as it appears to be generally true, that women are less modifiable than men? The relative conservatism of women—their greater adhesion to established ideas and practices—is manifest in many civilized and semicivilized societies. Is it so among the uncivilized? A curious instance of greater adhesion to custom by women than by men is given by Dalton, as occurring among the Juangs, one of the lowest wild tribes of Bengal. Until recently the only dress of both sexes was something less than that which the Hebrew legend gives to Adam and Eve. Years ago the men were led to adopt a cloth bandage round the loins, in place of the bunch of leaves; but the women adhere to the aboriginal habit—a conservatism shown where it might have been least expected. (265)

This curious instance reveals to Spencer both the savages' lack of modifiability and the special conservative nature of women. His intertwined arguments depend on the twin assumptions of female and savage inferiority. Indeed, he methodically develops a schema that simultaneously explains the position of women and savages. He relies on a metaphorical system in which each element depends on the other for its full meaning. In this system, the elements savage and woman interacted to evoke images of promiscuity and childishness. As Stepan (1993) argues, the system depended on prejudices of and fears about health and disease, sexual behavior, and moral development. The science of human variation helped calm these fears of out of control women and people of color by explaining perceived differences.

Explanations, such as those put forth by Spencer, came from the imaginary structure of Western, male-dominated concepts of primitives and lowly women. The building blocks of human science at the time were the racism and sexism of everyday life. Scientists such as Spencer and even Darwin pointed to the world they thought they understood to explain the unknown, and this known world included inferior creatures—women and savages.

The analogies used allowed for much slippage: In one *Popular Science Monthly* article or one section of *The Descent of Man*, the known part of an argument could move from race to gender. Thus, the relationship between the two seemed organic and, indeed, became organic. Even as our society turns away from biology toward other explanatory models, such as physics, the organic relationship between race and gender remain with us.

Notes

Epigraph: The quotation from Sigmund Freud appears on pp. 34–35 in *The Standard Edition of the Complete Psychological Works of Sigmund Freud*, translated and edited by James Stachey (London: Hogarth Press, 1953).

1. Ronald T. Takaki's *Iron Cages* (1979) makes a compelling argument, exposing the relationship between growing white supremacy, industrialization, and U.S. expansion into the Pacific and Central America. I would take this argument a step further by pointing to the antifeminist activity

that was raging during the second half of the nineteenth century. This is an important amplification because, as I argue later in this chapter, the debates about feminist projects, such as education and voting rights for women, not only paralleled but also often depended on prevailing notions of race.

2. Delauney is possibly Dr. Gaetan Delauney of France.

3. The question here is not simply whether or not this passage is an accurate description of Burmese gender relations. As Said (1978) points out, the Western discourse on the East does not rely on lies and myths alone. The abundance of the descriptions and the ability of Westerners to comment critically serve to freeze the East in a dependent position.

3 Africa on My Mind

Gender, Counterdiscourse, and African-American Nationalism

Equality is false; it's the devil's concept. Our concept is complementarity. Complementarity means you complete or make perfect that which is imperfect.

The man has the right that does not destroy the collective needs of his family.

The woman has the two rights of consultation and then separation if she isn't getting what she should be getting.

—Karenga, *The Quotable Karenga*

The African past lies camouflaged in the collective African-American memory, transformed by the middle passage, sharecropping, industrialization, urbanization. Few material goods from Africa survived this difficult history, but Africans preserved a memory of how social relations should be constructed that has affected African-American culture through the present. Although the impact of this

Portions of this chapter were published by Indiana University Press in E. Frances White, "Africa on My Mind: Gender, Counter Discourse and African-American Nationalism," *Journal of Women's History* 2, no. 1 (1990).

117

African heritage is difficult for historians to assess, today few deny its importance to African-American culture.

The memories I seek to interrogate in this chapter, however, have little to do with "real" memories or actual traditions that African Americans have passed along through blood or even practices. Rather, I explore the way African Americans in the late twentieth century constructed and reconstructed collective political "memories" of African culture to form a cohesive structure to shield them from racist ideology and oppression. In particular, I consider the political memories of African gender relations and sexuality that act as models for African-American social relations.

In the following pages, I focus on black nationalism as an oppositional strategy that both counters racism and constructs conservative utopian images of African-American life. I pay particular attention to the intertwined discussions of the relationship of the African past to present day culture and to attempts to construct utopian and repressive gender relations. Next I situate my work theoretically. Then I return to an examination of Afrocentric paradigms that support nationalist discourse on gender and the African past. Finally, I look at the emergence of a black feminist discourse that attempts to combine nationalist and feminist insights in a way that counters racism but attempts to avoid sexist pitfalls.

Throughout this chapter, I choose examples from across the range of nationalist thinking. Some of these writings are obviously narrow and sexist. Other works have influenced my thinking deeply and have made significant contributions to the project of understanding African-American women's lives. I argue, however, that all of these texts fail to confront the sexist models in which they are grounded. I imagine that my criticisms may be read by some as a dismissal of all Afrocentric thinking, but nothing could be further from my intentions. It is because I value the contributions of nationalists that I want to engage them seriously. Yet it is the kind of feminism that demands attention to internal community relations that leads me to interrogate this discourse even while acknowledging its ability to undermine racist paradigms. This is a black feminism that recognizes both the dangers of criticizing internal relations in the face of racist attacks as well as the risk of our failure to transform ourselves into a liberated community if we do not engage in dialogue on the difficult issues that confront us (see Clarke 1983, 1999; Lorde 1984).

African-American nationalists have taken the lead in resurrecting and inventing African models for the African diaspora in the United States. They recognize that the dominant images of Africa are negative representations that have justified black enslavement, segregation, and continuing impoverishment.[1] Accordingly, nationalists have always argued persuasively that African Americans deny their connections to Africa at the peril of allowing a racist subtext to circulate without serious challenge. At the same time, nationalists have recognized that counterattacks on negative portrayals of Africa stimulate political mobilization against racism in the United States. The consciously identified connections between African independence and the U.S. civil rights movements and, more recently, between youth rebellion in South Africa and campus unrest in the United States in the 1980s stand out as successful attempts to build a pan-African consciousness.

The construction of pan-African connections can have its problems, however. At times it requires searching for a glorious African past while accepting dominant European notions of what that past should look like. As I have argued before (E. White 1987a), proving that Africans created "civ-ilizations" as sophisticated as those in Europe and the Near East has concerned nationalists too much (see Diop 1974; C. Williams 1974). In the process of elevating Egypt, for exam-ple, nationalists have often accepted as uncivilized and even savage the majority of Africans who lived in stateless soci-eties, denying them the respect they deserve for the complex relationship they maintained with the world around them.

Perhaps more important, the nationalist or Afrocentric con-struction of a political memory attempts to set up standards of social relations that can be both liberating and confining. Ron Karenga, "inventor" of Kwanzaa traditions, illustrates this point by stating that "man has the right that does not destroy the collective needs of his family" and "woman has the two rights of consultation and then separation if she isn't getting what she should be getting" (quoted in Allen 1970:69). Build-ing on conservative concepts of "traditional" African gender relations before colonial rule, he argues that the collective needs of black families depend on women's complementary and unequal roles. As I illustrate later, Karenga has signifi-cantly modified his sexist ideas about gender relations, but the ideology of complementarity and collective family needs continues to work against the liberation of black women.

In addition, many nationalists, both male and female, remain openly hostile to any feminist agenda. In an article arguing that black people should turn to African polygamous and extended family forms to solve the "problem" of female-headed households, Larry Delano Coleman concludes:

> The "hyper-liberated" black woman is in fact so much a
> man that she has no need for men, however wimpish they

may be; and the "hyper- emasculated" black man is so much a woman, that he has no need for women. May each group of these hyper-distorted persons find homosexual heaven among the whites, for the black race would be better served without them. (1983:6)

Coleman defines "the race" in a way that excludes feminists, lesbians, and gay men from community support—a terrifying proposition in this age of resurgent racism.

In advocating polygamous families, Nathan and Julia Hare, the influential editors of *Black Male/Female Relationships,* link homosexuality with betrayal of the race:

Just as those black persons who disidentify with their race and long to alter their skin color and facial features to approximate that of the white race may be found to suffer a racial identity crisis, the homosexual individual who disidentifies with his/her biological body to the point of subjecting to the surgery of sex-change operations similarly suffers a gender identity confusion, to say the least. (1981:10)

Both the Hares' and Coleman's standards of appropriate gender relations depend on a misguided notion of African culture in the era before "the fall"—that is, before European domination distorted African traditions. These nationalists have idealized polygamous and extended families in a way that stresses both cooperation among women and male support of wives but ignores cross-generational conflict and intrafamily rivalry also common in extended, polygamous families. They have invented an African past to suit their conservative agenda on gender and sexuality.

In appealing to conservative notions of appropriate gender behavior, African-American nationalists reveal their ideological ties to other nationalist movements, including those of European and Euro-American bourgeois nationalists over the past two hundred years. These parallels exist despite the different class and power bases of the movements. European and Euro-American nationalists turned to the ideology of respectability to control sexual behavior and gender relations. This ideology helped the bourgeoisie create a "private sphere" that included family life, sexual relations, and leisure time. Respectability set standards of proper behavior at the same time that it constructed the very notion of private life. Nationalism and respectability intertwined as the middle class used the nation-state to impose its notions of the private sphere's proper place on the upper and lower classes. Through state-run institutions, such as schools, prisons, and census bureaus, the bourgeoisie disciplined people and collected the necessary information to identify and control them (see Mosse 1985).

Often African Americans have served as a model of abnormality against which nationalism in the United States is constructed. White bourgeois nationalism has repeatedly portrayed African Americans as a threat to respectability. Specifically, white nationalists have described both black men and women as hypersexual. In addition, black family life has consistently served as a model of abnormality. Black families were matriarchal both when the ideal white family was considered to be male dominated and now, when the white ideal has become a family headed by an equal heterosexual pair.[2]

As I have suggested, black people have developed African-American nationalism as an oppositional discourse to counter such racist images. Ironically, though not surprisingly, this nationalism, too, draws on the ideology of respectability to develop a cohesive political movement. But the African-

American ideology of respectability does not always share the same moral code as the ideology of Western nationalism. Some Afrocentric thinkers, such as Coleman, turn to Africa for models of gender relations and call for polygamy as an appropriate form of marriage between black men and women. More crucially, black nationalists did not and cannot call on state power to enforce their norms. Their opposition to abortion, for example, carries very different weight from the campaign of the Christian Right, whose agenda includes making a bid for control of state institutions.

It is African-American nationalists' lack of access to state power and their advocacy of an oppressed people that gives Afrocentric ideology its progressive, radical edge and ultimately distinguishes it from European and Euro-American bourgeois nationalism. Paradoxically then, Afrocentric ideology can be radical and progressive in relation to white racism and conservative and repressive in relation to the internal organization of the black community. Clearly, nationalists struggle in a way that can deeply threaten white racism. Both the open repression of and the ideological backlash against black nationalists indicate that their discourse strikes at the heart of black oppression. Yet I often find too narrow black nationalist efforts to define what the community or nation should be.

The Dialectic of Discursive Struggle

How does one prove strength in oppression without overstating the case, diluting criticism of the system and absolving the oppressor in the process? Likewise, the parallel dilemma is how does one critique the system and state of things without contributing to the victimology school which thrives on litanies of lost battles and casualty lists, while omitting

victoriesand strengths and the possibilities for change inherent in both
black people and society?

—Karenga, *Introduction to Black Studies*, 213

Karenga has identified a key dilemma facing black scholarship: How do black scholars take into account the possibilities of liberation at the same time that they balance a sense
of strength against the realities of victimization? One strategy
for moving beyond this dilemma to what Karenga calls an
"emancipatory Black science" (213) is to examine the ideological battles in which black people engage, exploring both
the racist discourse that they struggle against and the oppositional narratives constructed in the process of this struggle.
As a site of ideological battles, discourses intertwine with the
material conditions of our lives. They help organize our social
existence and social reproduction through the production of
signs and practices that give meaning to our lives (see Terdiman 1985). Closely tied to the socioeconomic and political
institutions that enable oppressive relationships, discourses
are embedded in a variety of forms. For example, the dominant discourse on Africa is a multilayered composite drawn
from scholarly literature, fiction, art, movies, television, the
media, travel books, government documents, folklore, jokes,
and more. The result is an image of Africa that reinforces the
continent's subordinate power relations to the West. Dominant discursive practice depends on more than lies and
myths, although misrepresentation and deception certainly
have roles to play in its strategy. Instead, the West's will to
gain knowledge about Africa has been inextricably bound up
with imperialist relations.

It is impossible for people's thoughts on Africa to be unencumbered by this discourse. None of us—not even Africans—

can come to the study of Africa without being influenced by its negative image. Accordingly, the effect of dominant discourse is to blind both the oppressor and the oppressed by setting up smoke screens between people and reality. As Said's *Orientalism* argues in regard to the Middle East, "for a European or American studying the Orient there can be no disclaiming the main circumstance of his actuality: that he comes up against the Orient as a European or American first, as an individual second" (1978:2). In this process a smoke screen emerges that allows arbitrary categories to appear natural and normal. For example, it makes us think that race is a natural category by taking minor biological differences and infusing them with deep symbolic meanings that affect all our lives. Race, then, is a social construction that feels real to us and has significant consequences.

The popular literature that influences even nationalists is peppered with images of primitive natives confronting European civilization. These natives build huts rather than houses; meanwhile, similar-looking structures in England are called picturesque cottages. By nature, natives divide themselves into tribes, whereas more sophisticated people form ethnic groups. These words—"tribe," "hut," "native," "civilization," and "primitive"—form a cluster that helps build a discourse placing Africans in a time warp outside the present. Not surprisingly, this cluster of words has a history in the anthropological vocabulary that supported imperialism, a vocabulary that anthropology has since discarded but that remains in popular usage. Many of these words can be found in Raymond Williams's *Keywords: A Vocabulary of Culture and Society* (1976), since the Western discourse on Africa is as much about Europe as it is about Africa—an exploration of what Africa is and, therefore, what Europe is not.

As Johannes Fabian (1983) has argued, the cluster of words surrounding Africa fixes "natives" in a time other than our own complex, contemporary era. Natives are primitive in the sense that they came first, living as Western ancestors lived in a simpler age. Even the word "tribe" suggests an earlier time, since Europeans were said to have belonged to them only in the distant past. The *Oxford English Dictionary* reminds us that a tribe is "a primary aggregate of people in a primitive or barbarous condition, under a headman or chief." "Tribe," then, suggests a notion of ethnicity that is more fixed than social relations have ever been in Africa.

The concept of fixed, static tribes suited the interests of colonial rulers, who sought to categorize and control Africans. "Tribe" continues to feed off the racist cluster of words that speak to us through films (*Tarzan* and its popular imitation, *The Gods Must Be Crazy*); magazines *(National Geographic* and related PBS specials); and newspapers *(New York Times* reports on tribal massacres in Burundi and Sierra Leone). The smoke screen created by words central to this racist discourse casts a thick pall over Africa.

And yet alternative voices emerge. Unfortunately, many influential works, such as Said's *Orientalism* (1978), have failed to account adequately for the development of the oppositional strategies that reveal contradictions in the dominant discourse. Admittedly, even those who consciously reject hegemonic ideology or who appear to live unencumbered by it cannot go untouched by its power. But the existence of resistance suggests a need to recognize the interrelationship between dominant discourse and counterdiscourse. I have followed Richard Terdiman's lead in focusing on the inseparably intertwined nature of hegemonic and oppositional discursive practices. In his "celebration" of counterdiscourse he suggests, "We might thus posit something like a Newton's Law in the discursive realm: for every dominant discourse a contrary and transgressive counter discourse" (1985:65). And he puts it more tersely: "No discourse is ever a monologue" (36).

The very nature of dominant discourse leads it to be contested by subordinate groups whose daily experiences help penetrate and demystify its hegemony.[3] This "dialectic of discursive struggle" reveals the vulnerabilities of hegemonies (Terdiman 1985:68). As part of the same dialectic, counterdiscourses operate on the same ground as dominant ideology. Scott argues:

> The crucial point is rather that the very process of attempting to legitimate a social order by idealizing it always provides its subjects with the means, the symbolic tools, the very ideas for a critique that operates entirely within the hegemony. For most purposes, then, it is not at all necessary for subordinate classes to set foot outside the confines of the ruling ideals in order to formulate a critique of power. (1985:338)

As I argue later, African-American nationalist contestation over the image of Africa often unconsciously accepts many of the terms of dominant discursive strategies, even when it attempts to move beyond the limits set by racist ideology.

In *Marxism and the Philosophy of Language*, V. N. Volosinov examines the struggles between dominant discourses and counterdiscourses as a contest over ideological signs. A sign stands for something lying outside itself. It does not "simply exist as a part of a reality—it reflects and refracts another reality. Therefore, it may distort that reality or be true to it, or may perceive it from a special point of view, and so forth"

(1973:10). For Volosinov, words are often a starting place to understand social relations. Unlike other ideological signs, "the entire reality of the word is wholly absorbed in its function of being a sign. A word contains nothing that is indifferent to this function, nothing that would not have been engendered by it. A word is the purest and most sensitive medium of social intercourse" (14).

Words, like all signs, evolve only on "interindividual territory," that is, between individuals. Thus, Volosinov stresses the "multiaccentuality" of the ideological sign (1973:23). Caryl Emerson explains:

> Each social group—each class, profession, generation, religion, region—has its own characteristic way of speaking, its own dialect. Each dialect reflects and embodies a set of values and a sense of shared experience. Because no two individuals ever entirely coincide in their experience or belong to precisely the same set of social groups, every act of understanding involves an act of translation and a negotiation of values. It is essentially a phenomenon of interrelation and interaction. (1986:185)

As Volosinov, Terdiman, and others have argued, language reflects the struggles between dominant and dissident discourses. Hazel Carby expresses this view: "The sign, then, is an arena of struggle . . . ; the forms that signs take are conditioned by the social organization of the participants involved and also by the immediate conditions of their interactions" (1987:17). In the case of interest to us, the meaning of Africa—the ideological sign *Africa*—is contested on discursive terrain. Dominant discourse assigns a plethora of negative images to Africa, while those influenced by nationalist impulses in Africa and its diaspora struggle to replace these images with their own positive meanings.

Yet, as suggested earlier, this counterdiscourse has a double-edged nature. In part because, as Emerson says, no two individuals "belong to precisely the same set of social groups" (1986:185), counterdiscourse struggles against both dominant and competing oppositional discourses. African-American nationalists attempt to protect themselves from negative images at the same time that they try to set the terms of appropriate behavior within the black community. Terdiman and Scott, both of whom write persuasively about the ways counterdiscourse can penetrate the contradictions inherent in dominant discourse, fail to examine the significance of alternative worldviews for the subordinated communities that project them as a defense against oppression. Scott, for example, seems unaware that poor men and women in the Malaysian village he studied might have competing interests. Neither Scott nor Terdiman recognizes the ways gender intersects with class and ethnicity to form overlapping and often contradictory social groups.

The writings of certain feminists of color reveal the Janus-faced nature of counterdiscourse as these women search for allies among the male-dominated nationalist and white-dominated feminist movements. For example, women of color have offered challenges within the feminist movement that have forced some white women to acknowledge the problems with the undifferentiated category "woman." Many of these theorists highlighted the complexities of human identity in recognition of the reality that women have ethnic/race and class positions, inter alia, that interact with gender and sexuality to influence their lives. Accordingly, feminists of color have pushed for a movement whose discursive practices oppose sexism and racism simultaneously. For example, Audre Lorde (1984) has asked: How does horizontal hostility keep women from ending their oppression? She has argued that women need to celebrate their differences and use difference for creative dialogue. Outside a narrow band of bourgeois or separatist feminists, few U.S. white feminists today write without giving at least token acknowledgment to Lorde's call to recognize difference.

At the same time, women of color have challenged their various ethnic communities to become conscious of sexism at home. Cherríe Moraga problematizes the meaning of home and community as she sensitively explores the way her education and light skin pushed her away from other Chicanos. "I grew white," she acknowledges (1983:99). But she also stresses that her community forced her to leave home because of her feminism and lesbianism. Feeling betrayed by a mother who accepted the ideology that males were better than females, she fled from those who told her that you are a traitor to your race if you do not put men first. She watched the rise of the Chicano nationalist movement, La Raza, alienated on the sidelines. Yet she found herself increasingly uncomfortable in her nearly all-white surroundings.

Ultimately, Moraga concluded that to be critical of one's race is not to betray it. She joined with other Chicana feminists to turn around the traditional interpretation of the life of the Aztec Malinche, which traces the birth of the Mexican people to Malinche's betrayal of her people to the Spanish conquerors. Instead, Moraga and others exposed a prior betrayal of Malinche, who had been sold into slavery by her own people.[4] By refusing to accept the terms of a Chicano nationalist movement that brands Moraga a traitor because she publicly criticizes gender relations, she demands a place for herself and other lesbians within Chicano communities.

It is not surprising that feminists such as Lorde and Moraga challenge both feminist and nationalist communities. As women with strong lesbian political consciences, they have confronted homophobia in nationalist movements. Locked in struggle against heterosexism in their own communities, it would have been very difficult for them to maintain an image of their communities as harmonious. Cheryl Clarke has specifically accused nationalists of increasing the level of homophobia in African-American communities during the 1960s and 1970s. She argues persuasively that homophobia limits the political struggle of African Americans:

> The expression of homophobic sentiments, the threatening political postures assumed by black radicals and progressives of the nationalist/communist ilk, and the seeming lack of any willingness to understand the politics of gay and lesbian liberation collude with the dominant white male culture to repress not only gay men and lesbians, but also . . . a natural part of all human beings, namely the bisexual potential in us all. Homophobia divides black people as political allies, . . . cuts off political growth, stifles revolution, and perpetuates patriarchal domination. (1983:207)

In *Reconstructing Womanhood*, Carby goes even further when she finds fault with some African-American feminists for failing to recognize that even their writings form part of a multiaccented counterdiscourse. She cautions black feminist literary critics to be historically specific when they write about black women's fiction and to recognize competing interests among African-American women. She asserts, "In these terms black and feminist cannot be absolute, transhistorical forms (or form) of identity" (1987:17). Black feminists do not have an essential, biologically based claim on understanding black women's experience, since we are divided by class, region, and sexual orientation. Even we have multiple identities that create tensions and contradictions among us (see Chapter 1 herein). We need not all agree, and we need not all speak with one voice. As with all counterdiscourses, the assumption that there exists one essential victim suppresses internal power divisions. To Terdiman's comment "No discourse is ever a monologue," we should add: The site of counterdiscourse is itself contested terrain.

Inventing African Tradition

The contemporary African-American woman must recognize that, in keeping with her African heritage and legacy, her most important responsibilities are to the survival of the home, the family, and its children.

—Charlyn A. Harper-Bolton,
"A Reconceptualization of the Black Woman," 42

It is out of the feminist tradition of challenging the oppositional discourses that are meaningful to women of color that I interrogate the significance of black nationalism for African-American women's lives. Like Sylvia Junko Yanagisako, "I treat tradition as a cultural construction whose meaning *must* be discovered in present words no less than past acts" (1985:18). As I have suggested, the traditions revealed in black nationalist discursive practices are Janusfaced—turned toward struggle with oppressive forces and contesting for dominance within black communities.

This double-edged discourse is exemplified by Molefi Kete Asante's writings and the *Journal of Black Studies,* which he edits. Recognizing the importance of developing a counterdiscourse within the privileged arena of academia, Asante publishes a consistently high-quality journal. He is also responsible for developing the first doctoral program in African-American studies at Temple University in Philadelphia.

The focus of his work and his journal is Afrocentric, placing "Africans and the interest of Africa at the center of our approach to problem solving" (1987:8). By "African," he means both people from the African continent and from its diaspora. Although he has collapsed the distinction between African Americans and Africans, he avoids the traps many nationalists fall into when they posit a simplistic, mystical connection between Africa and African Americans. Unlike earlier nationalists who appealed to a natural, essential element in African culture, in an editor's note introducing a special issue of the *Journal of Black Studies* entitled "African Cultural Dimensions," Asante argues that culture "is the product of the material and human environment in which people live" (1977:123). He continues:

> As editor I seek to promulgate the view that all culture is cognitive. The manifestations of culture are the artifacts, creative solutions, objects, and rituals that are created in response to nature. Thus, the manuscripts which have been scrupulously selected for this issue are intended to continue the drama of cultural discussion of African themes. (123)

Africans, Asante argues, have constructed a culture that stands in opposition to Eurocentric culture. He develops a convincing critique of a Eurocentric worldview. For Asante, Eurocentric culture is too materialistic, and the social science that has evolved from this culture in academe too often assumes an objective, universal approach that ultimately suffers from positivism. He argues that neither Marxism nor Freudianism escape this shortcoming, though he acknowledges that the Frankfurt School's criticisms of positivism have influenced his work.

According to Asante, the task for African Americans is to move beyond the Eurocentric idea to a place where transcultural, Afrocentric analysis becomes possible. He cautions against using a Eurocentric model that accepts oppositional dichotomies as a reflection of the real world (1987). His critique of the positivist tendency to split mind and body is cogent. Unfortunately, his theory itself relies on a false dichotomy. Essentially, his categories of Afrocentric and Eurocentric form an untenable binary opposition: Europeans are materialistic, whereas Africans are spiritual; Europeans abort life, whereas Africans affirm it.

Asante is quite right to recognize the existence of a protest discourse that counters racist ideology. But he denies the way that these discourses are both multivocal and intertwined. As suggested previously, the dialectic nature of discursive struggle requires that counterdiscourses and dominant discourses contest the same ideological ground.

This point can be better understood by examining the roots of Asante's Afrocentric thought. He consciously builds on Negritude and authenticity, philosophies devised explicitly to counter racist ideology and develop nationalist cohesion. V. Y. Mudimbe (1985) has exposed the nature of the binary opposition used in the 1930s and 1940s by cultural nationalists who explored their difference as blacks. Leopold Senghor and Aimé Césaire and other Francophone Africans and African Caribbeans relied on the spiritual/materialistic dichotomy. Turned on its head, this is the opposition used against Africans during the late nineteenth century. As many have pointed out, this reversal of paradigms owed much to the celebration of the "noble savage" by such interwar European writers as Jean-Paul Sartre. Ironically, Western anthropologists, whom nationalists often disparage, also took an active role in this ideological flip. Anthropologists such as Michel Griaule and Melville J. Herskovits revealed to Western-educated intellectuals the internal coherence of African systems of thought. Equally important was the cross-fertilization of ideas between Africans, African Caribbeans, and African Americans. As a result of these three influences, "African experiences, attitudes, and mentalities became mirrors of a spiritual and cultural richness" (Asante 1987:89). Far from being cultureless savages, Africans had built the essence of spiritual culture.

This reversal of the racist paradigms of Africa accompanied and contributed to the growth of the nationalist movements that ultimately freed the continent from formal colonial rule. The nature of African independence reflects the double-edged character of this nationalism. On one hand, nationalism helped build the political coherence necessary to threaten European rule; on the other hand, it obscured class and gender divisions in a way that prevented them from being addressed fairly. Clearly, this nationalism shared much with a European brand of nationalism that envisioned a culture unequally divided along gender and class lines.

Similarly, Asante does little to take us beyond the positivism that he criticizes, and his schema assumes a universality as broad as the Eurocentric discourse he shuns. Moreover, the Afrocentric ideology he embraces depends on an image of black people as having a culture that has little or nothing to do with white culture. This is one of its major contradictions. On one hand, nationalists such as Asante have to prove to African Americans that Afrocentric ways are different from and better than Euro-American ways. Nationalists try to convince black people that they should begin to live their lives by this Afrocentric ideology. For example, some nationalists argue that African Americans should turn away from materialism to focus on the spiritual needs of the black community. Yet on the other hand, Asante and others argue that black culture is *already* based on an Afrocentric worldview that distinguishes it from EuroAmerican culture. Rather than being an ideology that African Americans must turn to, Afrocentric thought becomes inherent in black culture, and black people already live by these ways in opposition to dominant culture.

I argue instead that African-American culture constantly interacts with dominant culture. Of course, black people put their own special touches on the results of these inter-actions. Nonetheless, blacks and whites all live together in the same society, and culture flows in both directions. Like members of the dominant culture, most African Americans believe that spirituality has a higher value than materialism at the same time that most of these people pursue material goals. If materialism were not considered crass by dominant society, Afrocentric critique would have little value. It is also important to note the extent to which white culture is influenced by African Americans. At an obvious level, we see black influence on white music with the recent appear-ance of rap music on television and radio commercials. At a less obvious level, Afrocentric critiques compel hegemonic forces to work at covering the reality of racist relations. Far from being an ideology that has no relationship to Euro-centric thought, nationalist ideology is dialectically related to it.

What I find most disturbing about Asante's work is his decision to collapse differences among black people into a false unity that only a simplistic binary opposition would allow. The focus on similarities between Africans and

African Americans at the expense of a recognition of historical differences can only lead to a crisis once differences are inevitably revealed. Moreover, Asante's binary opposition cannot account for differences among Africans. Many eloquent African writers have warned of the problems that developed from accepting a false unity during the decolonization phase, which led to the transfer of local power from an expatriate elite to an indigenous one. Ngugi wa Thiongo, Sembene Ousmane, and Chinua Achebe have all warned us against the danger of failing to recognize difference.

And, of course, we cannot face sexism with this false unity, as Buchi Emecheta, Sembene Ousmane, and Mariama Bâ movingly show. In *The Afrocentric Idea*, Asante does tell us that, in addition to moving beyond the Eurocentric idea, we can develop a "post-male ideology as we unlock creative human potential" (1987:8). Yet he says nothing more about gender in the entire book. It is hard to believe that he intends this as a serious gesture toward black feminists. We must turn to other Afrocentric thinkers to understand more clearly what this discourse has to say about women.

Karenga, the founder of US (a black cultural nationalist group founded in the 1960s and based in Los Angeles), is among the most important nationalists that the *Journal of Black Studies* publishes. Some readers will remember him for his leadership role among cultural nationalists in ideological battles against the Black Panthers in the 1960s and 1970s and for his pamphlet *The Quotable Ron Karenga*. In *Black Awakening in Capitalist America* (1970), Robert Allen quoted a critical excerpt from Karenga's book, exposing its position on women and influencing many young black women (including me) to turn away from this nationalist position.

Perhaps the key word in Karenga's early analysis of utopian gender relations is "complementarity." In this theory, women's roles should complement those of men, and therefore both sexes would share the responsibilities of nation building. Of course, in this formulation, "complementary" does not mean "equal." Instead, men and women would have separate tasks and unequal power. Indeed, in much of Africa today, women give more to men than they get in return in their complementary labor exchange. This is not to suggest that African women are only victims in their societies; nonetheless, sexism based on a complementary model severely limits the possibilities in many women's lives.

It is important to note that Karenga has reformed his position on women. Apparently, he made effective use of the time he spent in jail during the 1970s by spending much of it studying. It was from his jail cell that he published influential pieces in *Black Scholar* and the *Journal of Black Studies*. In these articles, he began to articulate more clearly a critique of hegemonic culture, showing the impact of his readings of Georg Lukacs, Antonio Gramsci, Amilcar Cabral, and Sekou Touré. And though he does not address them explicitly, he begins to respond to black feminist critiques of his work. Indeed, I find the change in Karenga's position on women impressive. Although he remains mired in heterosexist assumptions and never acknowledges his change of heart, he has dropped his explicit arguments supporting the subordination of women. Despite his continued hostility to feminists, the new Ron Karenga argues for equality in the heterosexual pair (1982).

Unfortunately, too few nationalists have made this transition with Karenga. Male roles remain defined by conventional, antifeminist notions that fail to address the realities of black life. For example, articles in Nathan and Julia Hare's journal *Black Male/Female Relationships* consistently articulate such roles. Charlyn A. Harper-Bolton begins her journal contribution, "A Reconceptualization of the Black Woman," by examining "traditional African philosophy, the nature of the traditional African woman, and the African-American slave woman" (1982:32). She uses African tradition as her starting point, because she assumes an essential connection between the African past and African-American present: "The contemporary African-American woman carries within her very essence, within her very soul, the legacy which was bequeathed to her by the traditional African woman and the African-American slave" (40). She leaves unproblematized the African legacy to African Americans as she presents an ahistorical model of African belief systems that ignores the conflict and struggle over meaning so basic to the making of history. This model assumes the same dichotomy between harmonious spirituality and conflicting materialism that grounds the work of Asante and her major sources, John Mbiti (1970) and Wade Nobles (1974).

It is a peculiarly Eurocentric approach that recognizes conflict and competing interests in a Western context but not in an African one. Harper-Bolton never moves beyond the mistaken notion that Africans lived simply and harmoniously until the evil Europeans upset their happy lives. Ironically, as I have been arguing, this image of Africans living in static isolation from historical dynamics supports racist ideals and practices and conveniently overlooks the power dynamics that existed as much in precolonial Africa as anywhere else in the world. In addition, Harper-Bolton's model portrays African women as constituting a monolithic and undifferentiated category with no competing interests, values, and conflicts. The power of older women over younger women that characterizes so many African cultures becomes idealized in her valorization of the elders' wisdom in decision making. She too readily accepts the view of age relations presented by more powerful, older women, whose hidden agenda often is to socialize girls into docile daughters and daughters-in-law.

When Harper-Bolton turns to the legacy of slave women for contemporary African Americans, she owes a large, but unacknowledged, debt to the social science literature on African survivals in African-American culture. In particular, her work depends on the literature that explores the African roots of African-American family patterns. Writers such as Herbert Gutman, John Blassingame, and Allan Kullikoff have attempted to build on Herskovits's early work on African survivals. This literature has been crucial for our understanding of black women's roles during slavery, particularly with reference to the African roots of these roles.

Unfortunately, the literature also shares certain problems that have clouded our understanding of this African heritage. Most worrisome are the sources these historians use to compare African and African-American slave families. Two major sources that have been used uncritically are particularly problematic in the study of the roles of precolonial African women. First, historians have relied on the accounts of precolonial travelers—Westerners who explored the African continent. Although these accounts are important sources (and I have turned to them myself) they must be used with great care—because it is precisely at the point of describing African women and gender relations that they are most problematic. As I argue in Chapter 2, often debates among these travelers over whether African women were beasts of burden and whether they were sexually promiscuous spoke to debates raging in Europe at the time. Rosalind Coward (1983) has explored the eighteenth- and nineteenth-century Western obsession with gender relations around the world, in which Westerners assumed that these relations were a measure of civilization. Needless to say, because these travelers brought the sexist visions of their own society to bear on African gender relations, their writings must be put to careful use.

Even more worrisome, however, is the second major source used by historians looking for African legacies—anthropological reports written between the 1930s and 1950s. My interest here is not in joining the chorus of "anthropology bashing"—accusing it of being the most racist of the Western disciplines. (Historians, after all, did not believe that Africa even had a history; they rarely turned their attention to its study until the 1960s.) It is the use of anthropological accounts in the study of African history that is very troubling to me. Used uncritically, as these accounts most often are, they lead historians into the trap that assumes a static African culture. Anthropology can give us clues about the past, but given the dynamic cultures that I assume Africa had, these clues must be treated carefully.

Moreover, there is a particular problem in the use of these accounts for understanding African women's history. Most of the reports relied on were written in the mid-twentieth century, a time when anthropologists and the colonial rulers for whom they worked were seeking to uncover "traditional" African social relations. They were responding to what they saw as a breakdown in these relations, leaving the African colonies more unruly and, most important, more unproductive than they had hoped to find them. Young men and young women were running off from the rural areas to towns, escaping the control of their elders. Divorce soared in many areas. The elders, too, were concerned with what they saw as a deterioration in their societies. Both elders and colonial rulers worried about young people getting married without their elders' approval and then—finding that they had chosen partners with whom they were no longer compatible—divorcing without approval and making new, short-term marriages.

The anthropologists set out to find out what had led to this "breakdown" and what were the customary rules that they saw as having restricted conflict in "traditional" Africa. Once again, we see emerging the concept of a harmonious Africa before the imposition of colonial rule. In A. R. Radcliffe-Brown's introduction to the seminal collection *African Systems of Kinship and Marriage*, he expressed this concern:

> African societies are undergoing revolutionary changes, as the result of European Administrators, missions, and economic factors. In the past the stability of social order in African societies has depended much more on the kinship system than on anything else. . . . The anthropological observer is able to discover new strains and tensions, new kinds of conflict, as Professor [Meyer] Fortes has done for the Ashanti and Professor Daryll Forde shows for the Yako. (Radcliffe-Brown and Forde 1950:84–85)

In part, Radcliffe-Brown and his co-editor, Daryll Forde, offered this set of essays as a guideline to colonial administrators so that the colonialists could counteract the destabilizing influences of Westernization. Such anthropologists obviously felt the need for a better understanding of people under colonial rule.

Not surprisingly, it was the male elders—not the junior women and men who were now getting divorced at an increased rate—whom the anthropologists asked about these customary laws. In "Making Customary Law: Men, Women, and Courts in Colonial Northern Rhodesia," Martin Chanock points out that customary law was developed out of this alliance between the colonial rulers and the elders. Of course, African elders were unequal partners in this alliance. Yet since both elders and colonial rulers viewed the increasing rates of divorce and adultery as signs of moral decline, they collaborated to develop customary laws to control marriages. "For this purpose claims about custom were particularly well-suited as they provided the crucial and necessary legitimation for the control of sexual behavior" (Chanock 1982:60). Chanock shows the way customary laws in Northern Rhodesia represented increased concern with punishing women to keep them under control. In many cases, such as adultery, what became institutionalized as "tradition" or "custom" was more restrictive for women than it had been in the past.

It was thus with the concern of maintaining men's control over women and elders' control over their juniors that many anthropologists of the 1940s and 1950s explored "traditional" African culture. To read their sources into the past could lead us to very conservative notions of what African gender relations were about. Yet when Harper-Bolton presents as unproblematic a model of gender relations that fails to question women's allocation to a domestic life that merely complements male roles, she accepts these views uncritically (see Harper-Bolton 1982:38). And, by extension, she buys into an antifeminist ideology. She warns that rejection of African tradition leads women in two directions that are antithetical to healthy developments in African-American family life. In one direction, women can fall into loose sexual behavior by accepting Euro-American conceptions of woman and beauty.

In the other direction, women can become trapped in the pursuit of aggressive careers and a rejection of motherhood. Harper-Bolton argues:

> What happened to this African-American woman is that she accepted, on the one hand, the Euro-American definition of "woman" and attempts, on the other hand, to reject this definition by behaving in an opposite manner. Her behavior becomes devoid of an African sense of womanness. In her dual acceptance/rejection of the Euro- American definition of woman, this African-American woman, in essence, becomes a "white man." (41)

Can Nationalism and Feminism Merge?

Not all Afrocentric thinkers are so blatantly antifeminist as Harper-Bolton. Some African-American women have attempted to combine nationalism and feminism. As black feminists have sought an independent identity from dominant white bourgeois feminism, some have explicitly turned to Afrocentric ideology for their understanding of gender relations. These efforts stress that African-American women grew up in families that had roots in African experiences and were therefore fundamentally different from those described by white feminists. Such arguments recognize the need to search for solutions to sexism in black families by basing them on our own experiences and history.

One of the most successful attempts to rely on Afrocentric thinking comes from an influential school of thought known as African women's diaspora studies. This approach, which tries to reclaim the African past for African-American women, is represented best in the edited collection *The Black Woman Cross-Culturally* (Steady 1981) and in the text *Women in Africa and the African Diaspora* (Terborg-Penn, Rushing, and Harley 1987). These works have significantly raised the level of understanding of the connections among women in Africa and its diaspora. A number of the scholars published in these books have read extensively about black women around the world and have drawn bold comparisons. For them, women from Africa and the African diaspora are united by a history of "economic exploitation and marginalization manifested through slavery and colonization and . . . [in the contemporary period] through neocolonialism in the U.S." (Terborg-Penn, Rushing, and Harley 1987:8). Influenced by nationalist impulses, they criticize much of the earlier literature on black women for using a white filter to understand African culture. Further, they persuasively argue that too often black women are presented as one-dimensional victims of patriarchy or racism. Instead, these writers use African feminist theory to remove this white filter distorting African-American lives and to identify "the cosmology common to traditional African women who lived during the era of the slave trade" and who provided a common cultural source for all black women today (Terborg-Penn, Rushing, and Harley 1987:49; see also Steady 1981, 1987).

Filomina Chioma Steady is careful to point out that she does not want to romanticize African history, and she acknowledges that tensions and conflicts existed in Africa as they did elsewhere. Unfortunately, because neither Steady nor any of the contributors to *Women in Africa and the African Diaspora* explore any of these tensions and conflicts, they present an overwhelmingly harmonious picture. Neither do they clearly articulate the ways in which they intend to unearth the cosmology of Africans living in the era of the Atlantic slave trade. Their footnotes do not reveal any sources on this cosmology that go beyond the problematic anthro-pological reports that give a male-biased view of the past.

Although African women's diaspora studies takes us a long way, it reveals some of the same shortcomings I have criticized in the nationalist writings of Asante and Harper-Bolton. These feminists accept the ideology of complementarity as if it sig-nified equality. They rely on a notion of African culture that is based on biased anthropological reports of a static, ahistor-ical Africa. Finally, they construct a dichotomy between African feminism and Western feminism that depends on the Afrocentric spirituality/Western materialism dichotomy. Clearly, these writers advocate women's equality, but they find it much easier to address racism in the women's move-ment than sexism in black liberation struggles. In their attempt to combine Afrocentric and feminist insights, they recognize the importance of nationalist discourse for coun-tering the hegemonic ideology that seeks to confine African-American lives. Going beyond the conservative agenda that nationalists have constructed, however, would strengthen their advocacy of a feminist discourse.

In a special issue of *Signs* devoted to women of color, Patricia Hill Collins (1989) has produced one of the most persuasive attempts to combine Afrocentric thought and feminism. In the tradition of Asante, she recognizes the need to struggle for increased space for African-American scholars within the academy. Although she does not raise the issue explicitly, I read her article in the light of the nar-row-minded failure of many academic departments to take Afrocentric scholars seriously and to give African Ameri-cans tenure. In recognition of the serious work many women's studies programs must do to make their classrooms appeal to more than white, middle-class students, Collins tries to sensitize feminists to a worldview—one that is potentially at odds with narrow academic training—that their black students may bring with them to class.

Collins may go too far, however, when she tries to identify an essential black women's standpoint. For her, the black women's standpoint has evolved from the experiences of enduring and resisting oppression. Black feminist thought is interdependent with the distinctive, self-defined standpoint of African-American women (1989:750). At the same time, black feminist theory intersects with Afrocentric and feminist thought.

For Collins, both Afrocentric and female values emerge from concrete experience:

> Moreover, as a result of colonialism, imperialism, slavery, apartheid, and other systems of racial domination, Blacks share a common experience of oppression. These similarities in material conditions have fostered shared Afrocentric values that permeate the family structure, religious institutions, culture, and community life of Blacks in varying parts of Africa, the Caribbean, South America, and North America. (1989:755)

Similarly, she goes on to say that

> women share a history of patriarchal oppression through the political economy of the material conditions of sexuality and reproduction. These shared material conditions are thought to transcend divisions among women created by race, social class, religion, sexual orientation, and ethnicity and to form the basis of a women's standpoint with its corresponding feminist consciousness and epistemology. (755)

Thus, the contours of Afrocentric feminist epistemology include black women's material conditions and a combination of Afrocentric and female values. Indeed, Collins's Afrocentric feminist values share much with the essentialist cultural feminism of Carol Gilligan, including the ethic of caring and the ethic of personal accountability (see Gilligan 1982).

Collins builds on the black feminist insight that black women experience oppressions simultaneously. Unfortunately, she, too, remains mired in a false dichotomy that limits the value of this insight. For example, although Collins recognizes the importance of discussing class, she seems unable to keep class as a variable throughout her analysis. At times, she assumes that all white women are middle class and all black women are working class. She sets up working-class black women to comment on the lives of privileged white women:

> Elderly domestic Rosa Wakefield assesses how the stand-points of the powerful [white middle-class women] and those who serve them [low-income black women] diverge: If you eats these dinners and don't cook 'em, if you wears these clothes and don't buy or iron them, then you might start thinking that the good fairy or some spirit did all that. . . . Blackfolks don't have no time to be thinking like that. . . . But when you don't have anything else to do, you can think like that. It's bad for your mind, though."
> (1989:748–49)

Missing in such accounts is the position of middleclass black women and working-class white women. Although Collins recognizes that some black women have obtained middle-class status, in her view, all white women have class privilege. She admits that "African-American women do not uniformly share an Afrocentric feminist epistemology since social class introduces variations among Black women in seeing, valuing, and using Afrocentric feminist perspectives"

(758). She even acknowledges that black women's experiences do not place them in a better position than anyone else to understand oppression. Yet the quintessential black woman is one who has "experienced the greatest degree of convergence of race, class, and gender oppression" (758). Collins certainly does not raise the possibility that class differences may create tensions within the black sisterhood that she takes as unproblematic.

Ultimately, Collins falls prey to the positivist social science that she seeks to critique. She links positivist methodology to a Eurocentric masculinist knowledge-validation process that seeks to objectify and distance itself from the "objects" of study. Like Asante, Collins recognizes many of the shortcomings of mainstream social science research, such as the tendency to create false objectivity. Yet also like Asante, she falls into a positivist trap. In Collins's case, she brings her readers back to the possibility of universal truths: "Those Black feminists who develop knowledge claims that both [Afrocentric and feminist] epistemologies can accommodate may have found a route to the elusive goal of generating so-called objective generalizations that can stand as universal truths" (1989:773). Like most positivists, Collins never asks: Whose universal truths are these anyway? Her quest for universal truth will be doomed to failure as long as she accepts as unproblematic an Afrocentric sisterhood across class, time, and geography. Collins's truths depend on an Afrocentric ideology that suppresses differences among African Americans.

Like all oppositional discourses, the Afrocentric feminism of Collins, Steady, Terborg-Penn, and colleagues has multi-sided struggles. They compete for ideological space against the dominant discourse on Africa and its diaspora and within feminist and nationalist movements. The dialectics of discursive struggle links their work to dominant discourse and other competing oppositional voices. Both dominant discourses and counterdiscourses occupy some of the same contested terrain. Afrocentric feminists usefully reveal the almost inescapable tendency of nationalist discourse toward conservative agendas on gender and sexuality. At the same time, they reveal the strengths of nationalist ideology in its counterattack against racism.

Notes

Epigraph: The epigraph is quoted in Richard Allen, *Black Awakening in Capitalist America* (Garden City, N.Y.: Anchor Books, 1970), 168–69.

1. To prove this point, they need only refer to the racist scientific theory that the spread of AIDS to humans began in central Africa with people who ate [subtext: had sex with] green monkeys. Heralded by the popular and scientific media, this theory appealed to a white culture that still believes that black sexuality is out of control and animalistic. The scientific evidence contributed to the racist subtext of the anti-AIDS hysteria (see Hammonds 1986; Hammonds and Cerullo 1987).

2. According to George Mosse (1985), German nationalists defined as outsiders people who did not live up to the norms set up in terms of nationalism and respectability. By labeling homosexuals, prostitutes, Jews, and so on as perverts who lived outside the boundaries of acceptable behavior, nationalists helped build cohesion. Jewish men, for example, were said to epitomize all that was unmanly and unvirile. A good, manly German looked on suspiciously at Jewish men. Many of the newly evolving negative identities and classifications fused with the stereotypes of Jews. In this way, the rise of National Socialism was inextricably tied to the increase in anti-Semitism.

3. See Scott 1985. James C. Scott, however, may underemphasize the extent to which people are influenced by dominant hegemonies.

4. See also Alarcón 1981; Anzaldúa 1987.

4 The Evidence of Things Not Seen

The Alchemy of Race and Sexuality

> What intellectual feats had to be performed by the author or his critic to erase me from a society seething with my presence, and what effect has that performance had on the work?
>
> —Morrison, "Unspeakable Things Unspoken: The Afro-American Presence in American Literature," 12

Toni Morrison asks of literary discourse, "What are the strategies of escape from knowledge? Of willful oblivion?" (1989:11). She seeks to determine in what ways African-American presence gets erased from discussions of American literature. The erasure takes place on several levels: African-American literature is ignored or undervalued; Euro-American writers either fail to write black people into stories or when they do, use our presence to define whiteness; and when blacks are present in Euro-American literature, literary critics fail to recognize that presence.

In the first part of this chapter, I take the tools that Morrison has developed for understanding race in literary discourse and use them to explore homosexuality in our past and present discourses. Although I have no reason to believe that Morrison intended this use of her tools, I find them helpful in the exploration of certain complex questions that she has chosen not to pursue. In my view, this particular "escape from knowledge" has limited Morrison's own understanding of the ways that difference between Euro-America and African America is constituted as well as the multiple ways that African Americans have created a rich culture.

James Baldwin was among the first writers to refuse this escape from knowledge about the connection between homosexuality and race. In the second part of this chapter, I look at the price that Baldwin had to pay for daring to break the silence on black homosexuality. Along the way, I also examine the limitations of Baldwin's insights. This investigation in no way indicates that I see Baldwin as having failed in some way; rather, it shows the boundaries that he set up to be understandable attempts at self-protection.

When I first read Baldwin, I had no understanding of how difficult it must have been during his early career to imagine black male homosexuality. As I argue here, the enforced silence into which he wrote has roots as deep as slave times. Even Morrison, who imagines forced sexual acts on a chain gang in *Beloved* (1982), has the men of Sweet Home Plantation turn to animals rather than to each other for sexual relief. Now, why could they not have comforted each other? If we cannot imagine black men giving black men comfort, we narrow our options for fighting racism.

Morrison's Views

I have chosen to begin my exploration into race and heterosexuality by focusing on Morrison, the dean of black women writers, because of both the influence she has had on my own thinking and the self-consciousness that she brings to her historical novels and literary criticism. As I suggest in my article "Listening to the Voices of Black Feminism" (1983), the relationship between black women writers and black women historians is crucial for the development of black women's subjectivity. We help each other imagine the past. *Beloved* (1987) and *Jazz* (1992a), two of Morrison's historical novels, bring a richness to the past that we historians could never achieve alone. Morrison herself is quite conscious of the role she plays in helping us gain access to that past. She has identified herself within a tradition whose roots are in slave narratives and whose mission has been to establish the humanity of black people. About the principal motivations that led to the writing of slave narratives, Morrison says this:

> Whatever the style and circumstances of these [slave] narratives, they were written to say principally two things. One: "This is my historical life—my singular, special example that is personal, but that also represents the race." Two: "I write this text to persuade other people—you, the reader, who is probably not black—that we are human beings worthy of God's grace and the immediate abandonment of slavery." (1990:299)

Morrison reminds us that even as these writers of slave narratives attempted to represent the race, they dropped a protective veil over their interior lives. "In shaping the experience to make it palatable to those who were in a position to alleviate it, they were silent about many things, and they 'forgot' many other things. There was a careful selection of the instances that they would record and a careful rendering of those that they chose to describe" (1990:301).

Although Morrison places herself in the tradition of these slave writers, she recognizes that the passage of time has created different conditions for the late twentieth-century black (woman) writer. More than a century and a quarter after emancipation, we now have the freedom to peek behind the veil that literate African Americans drew over their lives. But to gain access to that veiled interior life of the enslaved, Morrison suggests, we have to make use of memories; recollections; and, most important, imagination. Thus, Morrison engages in what she calls "literary archeology":

> On the basis of some information and a little bit of guesswork you journey to a site to see what remains were left behind and to reconstruct the world that these remains imply. What makes it fiction is the *nature* of the imaginative act: my reliance on the image—on the remains—in addition to recollection, to yield up a kind of truth. (1990:302, my italics)

As Morrison implies, even the literary critic and the historian engage in acts of imagination; only the nature of this act differs from that of the fiction writer. We nonfiction writers, too, must dig up the remains of the past and also apply our imaginations. Otherwise, the oppressive limitations on representation in the past will continue to dominate.

Morrison is astutely aware of the narrative strategies that protected African Americans from scrutiny and yet managed to assert their presence. She has also written movingly about the attempts to erase this presence from our literary traditions and history. Her review of Western canon formation carries with it an anger that reminds us of the power struggle behind the academic canon debates. In "Unspeakable Things Unspoken" (1989), Morrison exposes the hollow-

ness of attempts by traditionalists to "maintain standards"—
that is, to keep African-American writers out of the canon.
She shows very clearly the way that the ever-contested
value "quality" "is itself the subject of much rage and is seldom universally agreed upon by everyone at all times" (2).

Morrison, however, does not simply want African-American writers included in the master canon; she also wants a
rereading of that canon to recognize the presence of Africanisms. By "Africanisms," she means "the denotative and con-
notative blackness that African peoples have come to signify,
as well as the entire range of views, assumptions, readings
and misreadings that accompany Eurocentric learning about
these people" (1992b:6–7).

Africanisms are figures of speech that help Americans
imagine the negative; the abnormal; the evil; or, by contrast,
their opposites—the positive, the normal, and the good.
They are useful tropes because they communicate so much
without explicitly signaling the author's meaning and without diffusing the power of that meaning in the process.
Thomas McLaughlin has provided a useful explanation of
the way such tropes or figures of speech work:

> Figures [of speech] convince, though, not by a strictly logi-
> cal presentation but by an appeal to the irrational, the part
> of the mind that delights in their multiple meanings and
> deep reassurances. Figures reassure our belief in dominant
> systems of thought in that they rely on accepted categories
> and analogies. In this sense figures appeal to our desire to
> possess an untroubled, self-evident truth. (1990:88)

Similarly, Africanisms appeal to, for example, often unconscious fears about African Americans deeply embedded in
this society. Alternatively, they can be used to conjure up

desire, freedom, individualism, and much more (Morrison 1992b). They can play such wide-ranging roles because of African Americans' centrality in the formation of American identity. From the beginning, we have symbolized the opposite of whiteness. To recognize the boundaries of freedom, for example, Euro-Americans used the changing meaning of black slavery. As Morrison suggests,

> Through the simple expedient of demonizing and reifying the range of color on a palette, American Africanism makes it possible to say and not say, to inscribe and erase, to escape and engage, to act out and act on, to historicize and render timeless. It provides a way of contemplating chaos and civilization, desire and fear, and a mechanism for testing the problems and blessings of freedom. (7)

In *Playing in the Dark* (1992b), Morrison exposes Africanisms in Euro-American literature and the collective white unconscious at the same time that she highlights the willful failure of literary critics to acknowledge their presence. Critics, she points out, have developed a discourse around the master canon that denies the centrality of race in this literature. Traditional literary criticism has constructed American literature as if it were universal and race neutral by failing to bring critical scrutiny to the obvious existence of the Africanism trope.

In the next two sections of this chapter, I explore two historical periods that have been the subjects of Morrison's novels: (1) the slave era, during which many of the issues that remain central to U.S. culture—such as the relationship between freedom and gender—first emerged, and (2) the 1920s, during which urban life began to dominate black culture. In examining these two periods and novels, I extend

Morrison's notions of erasures and the power of Africanisms to the topic of homosexuality.

Morrison's Blues

> We can agree, I think, that invisible things are not necessarily 'not-there'; that a void may be empty, but not a vacuum.
>
> —Morrison, "Unspeakable Things Unspoken: The Afro-American Presence in American Literature," 11

Morrison's work has helped those interested in race turn their attention away from an exclusive and isolated focus on blackness toward the simultaneous construction of whiteness and the interaction between the two. Morrison acknowledges the importance of reading African-American writers, but (as I have suggested) she also wants us to reread the "master" works with a new sensitivity. Additionally, she acknowledges the way that feminist literary criticism has transformed our readings of works in the master canon to include a focus on the construction of the "Whiteman."

I suspect that it is not incidental that Morrison seems unaware of a similar project that has been carried on in gay studies by such literary critics as Eve Sedgwick. In *Between Men*, Sedgwick helps us understand the importance of studying sexuality by reminding us that sexuality is an "especially charged leverage-point, or point for the exchange of meanings *between* gender and class (and in many societies, race), the sets of categories by which we ordinarily try to describe the divisions of human labor" (1985:11). Sexuality helps to establish difference among races and between genders.

Clearly, many black writers, critics, and historians have recognized the way that North American literature has used sexuality to establish difference between African Americans and Euro-Americans. Morrison herself makes a point of this. In *Beloved,* for example, the owners of the Sweet Home Plantation use the control of black women's sexuality to subjugate their enslaved black men. The violent assault against Sethe carries as much meaning as it does because her sexuality is violated:

> "After I left you, those boys came in there and took my milk. That's what they came in there for. Held me down and took it. . . . Them boys found out I told on em. Schoolteacher made one open up my back, and when it closed it made a tree. It grows there still."
> "They used cowhide on you?"
> "And they took my milk."
> "They beat you and you was pregnant?"
> "And they took my milk!" (1982:16–17)[1]

Sethe is much more concerned about the sexual violation she has experienced than about the horror of having her back lashed beyond recognition. Sexuality here functions as a trope for lack of freedom; in their sexual domination, whites exercise ultimate control over what the most basic freedom would render private and personal. Indeed, this violation is as important to Sethe's husband, Halle, as it is to her. Hiding out in the hayloft, Halle watches as the young white men suck his wife's breasts. Paul D, Halle's brother, informs Sethe of Halle's response:

> "The day I came in here you said they stole your milk. I never knew what it was that messed [Halle] up. That was it, I guess. All I knew was that something broke him. Not a one of them years of Saturdays, Sundays, and nighttime extra never touched him. But whatever he saw go on in

that barn that day broke him like a twig." (Morrison
1982:69)

Morrison does not limit her use of the trope of sexuality
to heterosexual relations. In a significant scene that is so
subtly written that some readers may miss its import, the
trope of homosexuality defines difference between the races.
Morrison describes in detail the daily rituals of a chain gang
on which Paul D finds himself. Each morning, the men
chain themselves together and then kneel, awaiting "the
whim of a guard, or two, or three":

> Chain-up completed, they knelt down. The dew, more
> likely than not, was mist by then. Heavy sometimes and if
> the dogs were quiet and just breathing you could hear
> doves. Kneeling in the mist they waited for the whim of a
> guard, or two, or three. Or maybe all of them wanted it.
> Wanted it from one prisoner in particular or none—or all.
> "Breakfast? Want some breakfast, nigger?"
> "Yes, sir."
> "Hungry, nigger?"
> "Yes, sir."
> "Here you go."
> Occasionally a kneeling man chose gunshot in his head as
> the price, maybe, of taking a bit of foreskin with him to
> Jesus. Paul D did not know that then. (1982:108–9)

Here Morrison uses homosexuality as a literary trope,
just as many white writers have used Africanisms. The rit-
ual of homosexual oral sex between master and slave clearly
marks the black male captive as enslaved and subjugated. To
paraphrase her account of the use of Africanisms, homosexuality here has a simplistic, though menacing, purpose to
establish hierarchic difference (1992b:63).

This is certainly a rare example of a black writer imagining a slave past that includes homosexual rape as a possibility. Indeed, without citing evidence, bell hooks expresses what seems to be the belief of many: "The sexism of colonial white male patriarchs spared black male slaves the humiliation of homosexual rape and other forms of sexual assault. While institutionalized sexism was a social system that protected black male sexuality, it (socially) legitimized sexual exploitation of black females" (1981:24). The implications of homosexual rape and its relationship to heterosexual rape are significant. Why have African-American intellectuals not explored this issue? With Morrison-like curiosity, we should ask why historians have presented the African-American past as if the only sexual concerns that black men had during slavery were castration and whether they could protect (and, for some, control) black women's bodies.[2]

I must admit that I, too, feel ambivalent about lifting the veil from the possibility of homosexual rape. After all, homosexuality has already had such bad press—why add to that by pointing to instances in which it would be seen as sordid and despicable? Admittedly, the acknowledgment of heterosexual rape during slavery does not make most people think that the entire institution and various practices of heterosexuality need to be condemned, so perhaps people would not jump to such conclusions about homosexuality either. But, of course, homosexuality and heterosexuality are not parallel and equal constructions: The latter depends on the former for its claim of normalcy.

In *Beloved*, Morrison partially lifts the veil from what must have been a terrifying experience—black men's loss of control over their *own* sexuality. As I have suggested, even to acknowledge the existence of homosexuality—especially of homosexual rape—speaks into a context heavily laden with heterosexist assumptions. (Morrison's heterosexist assumption is that *watching* Sethe's violation could drive Halle crazy, whereas the actual violation of Paul D seems less traumatic.)

Are there clues—or remains—that we could use to unveil more completely a homosexual past? We know that homosexual behavior was not foreign to the slave South. Martin Duberman's (1989) published correspondence between two southern white slave holders—Judge Jeff Withers, who helped draw up the government for the Confederacy, and large-plantation owner James H. Hammond, well known in local and national politics—implies a youthful homosexual relationship between the two men.

Duberman uses the clues from this correspondence and from Hammond's life to speculate that "sexual contact between males (of a certain class, region, time, and place), if not commonplace, was not wholly proscribed either" (1989:161). With irony, Duberman reminds us that "to date we have accumulated only a tiny collection of historical materials that record the existence of *heterosexual* behavior in the past. Yet no one claims that that minuscule amount of evidence is an accurate measure of the actual amount of heterosexual activity which took place" (161). Yet even Duberman, who has often written on African-American history, is strangely silent on cross-race homosexual activity. Perhaps he did not want to taint homosexuality by acknowledging that homosexual relationships, like heterosexual ones, can take place between unequals.

In contrast, Robert K. Martin has turned to popular literature of the mid-nineteenth century to show the ways that white male writers used Africanisms to create sexual danger in a text. In examining how men of color functioned in the homosocial world of these writers, Martin suggests that such nineteenth-century fictional male couples as Mandrake and Lothar and even the Lone Ranger and Tonto serve

> as a physical confirmation of what can only be suggested in the text, as the realization of male sexuality in a union with the dark and forbidden. To be a male homosexual is thus to couple with the devil, to embrace the primitive, for it was these figures that the African represented metonymically in the popular culture of the mid-nineteenth century. (1989:177)

In Theodore Winthrop's popular novel *Cecil Dreeme*, the main character, Byng, thinks to himself about his slave Densdeth, "I saw on the steamer that you were worth buying, worth perverting" (quoted in Martin 1989:177). Martin points out that Byng has managed to turn things around, to make it seem as if his slave Densdeth has control over him. Martin argues:

> For Byng finds himself here feminized, that is, read as the woman to be purchased and corrupted; but the presence of the concept of "perverting" makes it clear that this feminization is precisely what is feared in homosexual panic: the loss of male autonomy and power.
> To accept the embrace of Densdeth is to succumb to Densdeth's other self, the dark African, to accept, symbolically at least, anal penetration (entry into the darkness within) and thus to make oneself over as female, a commodity to be exchanged. (1989:177–78)

Martin brings together an understanding of Africanisms, homophobia, and sexism in a complex way. He takes these structures of dominance as literary tropes that depend on fears that were deeply embedded in the psyches of many nineteenth-century white men. Byng's relationship with Densdeth represents the possibility of homosexual desire between master and slave. In this perverse projection, the actual power relationship has been inverted; the master imagines himself as a woman dominated by his black slave. From the evidence of narratives like this, it would seem that black men certainly entered the homoerotic imagination of at least some white men. With such clues, it is not hard to imagine that some masters did in fact rape their enslaved black men.

Of course, I am not implying that homosexual rape was as widespread as heterosexual rape. I certainly do not want to be misread as suggesting that slave plantations and farms were gay dens of iniquity. What is important is the *potential* for homosexual rape rather than its actual prevalence. We need to ask why we persist in seeing the sexual emasculation of black men as stemming from their actual castration or their inability to protect black women from rape rather than also from their inability to protect *themselves* from rape.

And what of homosexual desire *between* black men? Is it unreasonable to ask that Morrison, Duberman, and other intellectuals imagine *that?* Male slave narratives are understandably silent on questions of sexuality. As Morrison explains, they were often silent about or "forgot" that which their intended audience would find intolerable to confront. Moreover, the struggle to transform oneself from a slave into a literary subject—to narrate one's story—was ultimately a bid for the power to assert one's humanity. For black men, the struggle to write and publish was symbolic of the act of establishing manhood. As Henry Louis Gates Jr. succinctly puts it, "The purported connection between the act of writing and the 'rights of man' did not escape the notice of the slave" (1985:xxvii). With the stakes so obviously high, we need not be surprised, then, that slave narratives reveal nothing about homosexual behavior. Since homosexual activity was seen as sinful, male slaves had reason to draw a veil over this life.

Given that Morrison has set herself the task of drawing back the veil from that life, I wish she had gone a step further. It strikes me as a failure of imagination that, in describing the relationships among the Sweet Home Plantation men, she sees no possibility that they might sexually comfort each other. We know enough about bisexuality among African-American men today to see that heterosexual desire does not preclude homosexual desire.

Morrison's narrative serves to undermine the old sexist belief that black men who watched their women get raped suffered more than these black women did. To my mind, she could have taken this effort further if she had been able to imagine more powerfully the sexual humiliation suffered by the men in her novel. Given the unequal power relationship between the Sweet Home masters and their enslaved men, she would have been able to explore more deeply the relationship between power and desire. Finally, if she had imagined African-American men comforting each other, she might have helped us think our history differently.

Representing the Renaissance

In moving from *Beloved* (1982) to *Jazz* (1992a), Morrison follows the great African-American migration from the former slave South to the urban North during the early twentieth century. Set during what many have called the Harlem Renaissance, *Jazz* places sexuality and gender at the center

of the struggles African Americans faced to build new communities in the North. In a book that points to both the
fragility and the necessity of community, characters flee
antiblack pogroms in the South and dodge antiblack riots in
the North, all the while searching for fulfilling relationships
with one another. There is a freedom in *Jazz* that we do not
see in *Beloved*—a freedom that includes the opportunity to
look for love and sex without the direct interference of the
masters. At one point, Morrison describes a party:

> It's good they don't need much space to dance in because
> there isn't any. The room is packed. Men groan their satis-
> faction; women hum anticipation. The music bends, falls to
> its knees to embrace them all, encourage them all to live a
> little, why don't you? since this is the it you've been look-
> ing for. (1992a:188)

Jazz is a music of improvisation—which is precisely the
skill African Americans used in order to adapt in the urban
North. Through the jazz idiom, Morrison helps us imagine
the emerging desires of the new urban working class. She
has her unnamed narrator tell us of the hopes that led
African Americans to Harlem:

> A city like this one makes me dream tall and feel in on
> things. Hep. . . . When I look over strips of green grass lin-
> ing the river, at church steeples and into the cream-and-
> copper halls of apartment buildings, I'm strong. Alone, yes,
> but top-notch and indestructible—like the City in 1926
> when all the wars are over and there will never be another
> one. The people down there in the shadow are happy about
> that. At last, at last, everything's ahead. The smart ones say
> so and people listening to them and reading what they
> write down agree: Here comes the new. Look out. There

goes the sad stuff. The bad stuff. The things-nobody-could-help stuff. . . . History is over, you all, and everything's ahead at last. (1992a: 7)

In *Jazz*, Morrison provides a wealth of vivid images of the past; but, again, her heterosexist bias limits her imagination. To paraphrase her words in another context (Morrison 1989:12), I wonder what intellectual feats she had to perform to erase the homosexual presence from the Harlem of the 1920s. It seems to me infinitely more difficult to escape from the knowledge of homosexuality when imagining the 1920s than when imagining the 1820s.

What clues has Morrison willfully overlooked? By the 1920s, gay communities were becoming increasingly visible in large cities (Chauncey 1994; Faderman 1991b). As I argue later, evidence suggests that African Americans participated in the sprouting of these communities, and Harlem blacks played a particularly prominent role in their development. Judging from the number of notable people who engaged in homosexual activity, I speculate that the great migration that brought so many African Americans north coughed up a number of "sexual deviants."

Work on blues singers of that era is instructive here. A number of recent writings (Faderman 1991a; Faderman 1991b; McCorkle 1997) have brought attention to the homosexual behavior of many famous blues singers, such as Alberta Hunter, Bessie Smith, and Ethel Waters. Hazel Carby (1986) sees such artists as folk heroes who helped African Americans make the transition from the rural South to the urban North. Carby notes that they spoke easily of sexual matters. Indeed, a number of their lyrics, such as Ma Rainey's "Prove It on Me Blues" and Lucy Bogan's "B.D. Women Blues," represented lesbian behavior and beliefs.

It would be a mistake to conclude, as many have, that the openness of some blues singers about homosexuality suggests that black communities were necessarily tolerant of homosexual behavior. After all, many conservative Christians saw blues singers as agents of the devil, and efforts to divert attention from open discussions of sexuality—heterosexual or homosexual—were surely not limited to the middle class. Nonetheless, the lyrics and the behavior of some blues singers clearly indicate the presence of homosexuality during the 1920s. Although blues singers did not represent the views of all African Americans, they were able to express some of the desires and discontent of an important minority of women precisely because, as "sexual perverts," these singers stood in an uneasy relationship to the community. This outsider status allowed them to comment so clearly on society.

Indeed, so many of the prominent blues singers engaged in homosexuality that perhaps we should hypothesize on the connection between "deviant" sexuality and cultural production. When we turn to the writers, artists, and other intellectuals of the 1920s, we find that a similarly large number engaged in homosexual activity. In *Color, Sex, and Poetry* (1987), Gloria T. Hull identifies the male homosocial network that dominated the Harlem Renaissance, crossing race boundaries. Indeed, the fact that Alain Locke was a misogynist homosexual was key to the functioning of the Renaissance; he preferred men as writers and as lovers, and his contacts with the white homosexual literary world were invaluable. Similarly, in the diaries and letters of women writers such as Alice Dunbar-Nelson and Georgia Douglas Johnson, Hull finds evidence of a female homosocial network that included women connected by homosexual desire.

Eric Garber (1990) also finds evidence of strong homosexual networks in the Harlem artistic scene. He details the importance of those networks for the white voyeurs who traveled to Harlem for sex and danger. Ironically, Garber, like earlier whites who associated blacks with sexual freedom, both fetishizes and objectifies the black homosexuals he describes.[3] Nonetheless, he helps us see the important role of both African-American culture in the formation of homosexual communities and of homosexuality in the formation of black communities. In Morrison's language, the Africanism of blackness represented sexual freedom. Not surprisingly, then, whites felt freer to explore homosexuality in communities where they could be sexually expressive with relatively few consequences. Black homosexuals became important models of how white homosexuals should act.

Thus, although it is true that conservative elements in the African-American community of the 1920s condemned most open expressions of sexuality, it is also true that homosexual and bisexual desires were clearly fighting for space and representation. Significantly, that space emerged among artists, both bourgeois and popular.

Morrison has chosen to ignore this struggle. *Jazz* explores so sensitively the challenges African Americans faced in forming heterosexual bonds in the urban North of the 1920s. Yet these were not the only bonds available to them. By failing to develop the possibility of homosexual bonds, here again Morrison leaves a veil over both the complexities of the black community's internal relationships and the relationships between blacks and whites. With our view thus obstructed, we can neither explore the problematic relationship between the emerging black

and white gay and lesbian communities nor fully understand the ways that race influenced these relationships.
Moreover, we cannot appreciate the full range of ways
that African Americans adapted to urban life. As they
struggled to escape the legacy of slavery and the realities of
southern segregation, they asserted control over their sexual lives. And for some, this control included the exercise
of homosexual desire.

Clearly, Morrison has made an impressive contribution to
American letters. Her criticism and fiction combine to speak
to long-standing debates about the nature of American society that have traditionally been dominated by white male
authors. And she has managed to add a black feminist voice
to these debates. In the process, among her many other
achievements, she exposes racism in the collective white
unconscious and shows the ways that sexuality can be used
to construct hierarchical differences between genders and
races.

Yet by failing to explore homosexuality more fully, Morrison has limited our understanding of the complex ways
sexuality is used. The history of blackness and the history of
sexuality are intertwined, and both heterosexuality and
homosexuality can act as leverage points for expressing the
unequal difference between whites and blacks. Given the
close relationship between race and sexuality, it seems
inevitable that the rise of homosexuality as an important
category and homophobia as a central preoccupation is also
bound to the history of blackness. Her many other contributions notwithstanding, Morrison's heterosexist project
leaves a heavy veil in place over this history.

Baldwin: Unspeakable Things Finally Spoken

It was James Baldwin who most created the space for a kind of male homosexual presence that had previously been unimaginable. As I argue shortly, this space was not uncomplicated, but it was fertile. To understand Baldwin's work on homosexuality, let us first turn briefly to his related views on race.

Baldwin was the first writer I encountered who gave brutally honest, nonfiction testimony to the impact of racism on aspiring, young black intellectuals. Several of his essays in *Notes of a Native Son* (1955) address his concern with escaping from being merely a "Negro" or even merely a Negro writer. When he wrote this book, I think he was only beginning to understand the many ways that *he* had accepted the word "Negro" as a term of diminishment.

Baldwin's response to racism's tendency to limit the complexities of his thinking and the complexities of what could be thought about him was to attack the racial categories that helped oppress him. In a famous article on Richard Wright, Baldwin argues that the concept of race, so central to understanding U.S. culture, also blinds us to certain conditions; our racial categories conceal what he considered to be truth.

Baldwin's insights are striking for their early breaks with race as an essential category. He often emphasized the barriers to insight created by racial categories. These categories allowed whites to project from their collective unconscious the fear and guilt they felt toward blacks.

I suspect that Baldwin's discomfort with being categorized as gay was partially fueled by this insight about race. Like a number of gay men from his generation, Baldwin struggled against such labels in an effort to persuade heterosexuals to focus on the similarities they shared. For him, heterosexual men, like homosexuals, had to learn to accept their desires in all their instability and fluidity; the task for both was to escape what Baldwin called the prison of masculinity. Thus, he sought to disrupt the category "man" by demonstrating that the binary straight/homosexual is a false one.

This concern about the similar problems faced by all men emerges in Baldwin's novels. The copy on the book jacket of the 1962 Dial Press edition of *Giovanni's Room*, Baldwin's most talked about book in the gay literary canon, is revealing. It says:

> *Giovanni's Room* is both a novel of extraordinary literary quality and a completely honest treatment—perhaps the most outspoken yet—of an extremely controversial theme: "David's dilemma," writes Mr. Baldwin, "is the dilemma of many men of his generation; by which I do not so much mean sexual ambivalence as a crucial lack of sexual authority."

To Baldwin, this book is not, as one might think, about homosexuality; rather, it is about the quest of all men to come to terms with their own desires.

Baldwin's attempts to explain and stress the similarities between homosexuals and heterosexuals occupied him throughout his writing career. In *Just above My Head*, he takes up this theme early in the book. Tony, the son of the narrator, Hall Montana, asks his father about the sexual orientation of his Uncle Arthur.

> [*Tony:*] "A lot of the kids at school—they talk about him."
> . . .

"They say—he was a faggot." . . .

[*Hall:*] "I know—before Jimmy—Arthur slept with a lot of people—mostly men, but not always. He was young, Tony. Before your mother, *I* slept with a lot of women . . . mostly women, but—in the army—I was young, too—not always. You want the truth, I'm trying to tell you the truth. . . . I'm proud of my brother, your uncle, and I'll be proud of him until the day I die. . . . Whatever the fuck your uncle was, and he was a whole lot of things, he was nobody's faggot."

"Tony—didn't me and your mother raise you right? didn't I . . . tell you, a long time ago, not to believe in labels?" (1979:36–37)

That Arthur slept with men does not distinguish him from straight men. Indeed, Baldwin's ideal homosexual man was one who lived in a heterosexual world despite his sexual attraction to other men.[4] For Baldwin, homosexuals were not marked by any significant difference, partly because he felt that we are all bisexual or androgynous in the sense that we all contain both male and female elements. Toward the end of Baldwin's life, in "Here Be Dragons," he returns to the topic of similarities among men. He concludes, "But we are all androgynous, not only because we are all born of a woman impregnated by the seed of a man but because each of us, helplessly and forever, contains the other—male in female, female in male, white in black and black in white" (1985:690).

Baldwin wanted to explain to the world and to himself that his attraction to men did not make him abnormal and certainly should not exile him from the race. This concern may have intensified as Baldwin's desire to be viewed as a race person grew and as he became increasingly immersed in the black liberation struggles of the 1950s and 1960s. In *No Name in the Street,* published in 1972, Baldwin talks about the effect of the

Civil Rights movement on his thinking. He began to understand the necessity for acknowledging, and even at times moving and writing from, rage. Although he continued to call on love as the ultimate means to avoid a racial holocaust, he no longer expected black writers to distance themselves from their feelings about racism. As I read his work, he seemed to be writing increasingly for black audiences rather than for white liberals.

Baldwin acknowledged that many of his new insights and attitudes came from younger men in the movement. Unfortunately, his bonds with these young black men were challenged by homophobia. Nowhere was this challenge more clear than in the famous confrontation between Baldwin and Eldridge Cleaver. In Cleaver's celebrated essay entitled "Notes on a Native Son," from *Soul on Ice*, he acknowledges that he initially found Baldwin's writings on race insightful but later began to think that Baldwin hated black masculinity. Cleaver uses Baldwin's brave revelations about racism's impact on his psyche—revelations that were meant to exorcise him of this affliction—to make Baldwin pay for his honesty and vulnerability. For Cleaver, Baldwin's homosexual desires were signs of his racial pathology. He argues that Baldwin's racial self-hatred led to a racial death wish— a bizarre desire that, in Cleaver's mind, also motivates black nationalists. "The attempt to suppress or deny such [homosexual] drives," writes Cleaver, "leads many American Negroes to become ostentatious separationists, Black Muslims, and back-to-Africa advocates" (1968:101).

For Cleaver, black homosexuality becomes the expression par excellence of a racial death wish:

> The case of James Baldwin aside for a moment, it seems that many Negro homosexuals, acquiescing in this racial

death-wish, are outraged and frustrated because in their
sickness they are unable to have a baby by a white man.
The cross they have to bear is that, already bending over
and touching their toes for the white man, the fruit of their
miscegenation is not the little half-white offspring of their
dreams but an increase in the unwinding of their nerves—
though they redouble their efforts and intake of the white
man's sperm. (1968:102)

Cleaver here makes his point through a gendered analogy: Homosexuals are failed men who must hate themselves.[5] Somehow, the betrayal of the black (male) homosexual is made to seem reminiscent of the mythical betrayal
of black women who slept with white masters and then
gave birth to mulatto children. For Cleaver, this kind of
racial self-hatred led Baldwin to criticize Richard Wright
because he "despised—not Wright, but his masculinity. He
cannot confront the stud in others—except that he must
either submit to it or destroy it. And he was not about to
bow to a *black* man" (1968:160). I suspect that Cleaver felt
that faggots were men who were penetrated—that is, they
were like women—whereas men who penetrated men
and/or women were real men. Moreover, as William J.
Spurlin speculates, Cleaver's anxieties about black gay men
and his feminization of Baldwin "raise for speculation
whether it was he or Baldwin who was the more eager for
the 'fanatical, fawning, sycophantic love [and acceptance] of
whites' (Cleaver [1968:]99)" (Spurlin 1999:114).

Baldwin's response to Cleaver was surprisingly restrained.
In *No Name in the Street,* he suggests that Cleaver is like a zeal-
ous watchman who fears that Baldwin has allowed the
Establishment to use him. But in essence, Baldwin maintains,
they agree: What threatens black masculinity is white power.

Baldwin hypothesizes that Cleaver has him "confused in his mind with the unutterable debasement of the male—with all those faggots, punks, and sissies, the sight and sound of whom, in prison, must have made him vomit more than once" (1972:171–72).

Of course, like his fictional character Arthur in *Just Above My Head,* Baldwin was no faggot. Clearly, he wanted to distance himself from the "debased" homosexuals of the prisons. Although understandable, this strategy was double-edged. To protect himself from vicious attack, Baldwin turned to a politics of respectability. *He* was a respectable man, even if homosexual. Baldwin wanted to separate himself from those homosexuals whose behavior proved them to be debased. This strategy, however, leaves too many exposed to homophobic disciplining. Moreover, it does not sufficiently undermine the homosexual/heterosexual binary because the category "man" depends on too many exclusions—including woman. These points have become increasingly clear in more recent years from gay studies and gay politics, both of which have been influenced by Baldwin's insights (see, for example, Harper 1999).

Ironically, it was Baldwin's own narrow vision of masculinity that left him exposed to attacks like Cleaver's. Baldwin could not defend himself as a man against the assertion that he was like a woman. Although, as he suggested in "Here Be Dragons" (1985), he believed that all males contain elements of the female, he devalued womanhood. And he made the mistake of allowing Cleaver to set the terms— terms that assumed that "woman" is an inherently diminished position. Baldwin never recognized heterosexuality's investment in the rigid and gendered boundaries for desire. By allowing the terms of masculinity to remain intact and gender to remain fixed, he had no recourse in the face of Cleaver's denigrating assaults. As long as gay men could be disparaged as failed men—as essentially women—Baldwin would have no comeback.

It is sadly ironic that in desiring members of his own sex, Baldwin risked losing the protection provided by the very men he so dearly loved. As he suggests in *Just above My Head* (1979), loving black men can be a revolutionary act in this racist society. Indeed, I have rarely read anyone else who writes so lovingly about black men; Baldwin wrote from a devotion to his brothers born of living their lives *and* holding them in his arms. Yet his love placed him outside the norms of both the dominant society and the black community. In *No Name in the Street* (1972), as he speaks affectionately of black militants such as Cleaver, Baldwin barely conceals the pain he must have felt at Cleaver's harsh indictment.

I had the chance to see Baldwin interact with younger black men from the Black Power movement. From 1982 until the end of his life, Baldwin was a Five College Faculty member in western Massachusetts. The first year of his appointment, he was based at Hampshire College, where I was on the faculty; he then moved to Hampshire's nearby consortial school, the University of Massachusetts at Amherst. Many of his associates were former members of SNCC and other black power organizations. Baldwin was famous for his traveling retinue; I figured I would fit right in. Much to my surprise, however, there did not seem to be much space for a black lesbian feminist.

Hints about why, beyond my own shy personality, I might have found Baldwin's space uncomfortable can be found in a dialogue between Audre Lorde and Baldwin that took place at Hampshire College in the fall of 1984. The transcript was excerpted in *Essence* magazine. Baldwin and Lorde disagreed early and often. I cannot help feeling that some of Lorde's anger was directed toward the way Baldwin tried to suppress his sexual difference even though Lorde spoke mostly of gender difference. Baldwin seemed—at first, anyway—to be looking for common ground, but Lorde, who had staked her reputation on exposing difference and hidden power, would have none of this:

> *Lorde:* Truly dealing with how we live, recognizing each other's differences is something that hasn't happened. . . .
>
> *Baldwin:* Differences and samenesses.
>
> *Lorde:* Differences and samenesses. But in a crunch, when all our asses are in the sling, it looks like it is easier to deal with the samenesses. When we deal with samenesses only, we develop weapons that we use against each other when the differences become apparent. And we can wipe each other out—Black men and women can wipe each other out—far more effectively than outsiders do. (Lorde and Baldwin 1984:74)

Lorde so clearly understands the ways that differences can be used against people even as these differences are being denied. Baldwin countered Lorde's arguments about difference by misrepresenting her: He maintained that she was trying to blame black men for the condition of black women and children. Finally, exasperated by Lorde's relentless and aggressive efforts to get through to him about difference and sexism, he cut her off with an angry retort: "But don't you realize that in this republic the only real crime is to be a Black man? . . . How can you be so sentimental as to blame the Black man for a situation which has nothing to do with him?" (Lorde and Baldwin 1984:133)

For Baldwin, black sexism flows from white racism. Obviously, in making the point that black women endure racism not simply as blacks but also as black women, Lorde has spoken past him. Baldwin showed no willingness to recognize the complex ways that categories such as race and gender intertwine.

The dynamic of the Baldwin/Lorde debate reveals Baldwin's resistance to the theoretical contribution of feminism and his commitment to male-dominated models for understanding race. Lorde was irrelevant to him; his interest was limited to relations among black men and between black and white men. He played out those interests in the largely male following that surrounded him in Amherst. In this context, I found myself uncomfortably suppressing my own concerns about sexism and homophobia. My concerns seemed to threaten the very fragile male bonds that kept his following together.

When I was around "Jimmy," I sensed the reconstruction of an elaborate closet. We all knew that there were so many ways in which Baldwin was out: He was regularly surrounded by men who were interested in him, and his fiction clearly spoke for him. But this kind of open homosexuality threatened the terms of masculinity and the politics of respectability in which many in his following were invested; somehow he needed to find a way for homosexuality to be recognized but ignored. What an enormous task! Manhood had to be constructed as if it were undifferentiated by sexuality and as if it stood for the race as a whole. Unfortunately, this homosexual panic created—and continues to create—real barriers to the prospect of black men comforting each other. As long as the African-American community colludes in an escape from knowledge about black homosexuality, this kind of caring must remain in the closet.

My comments about Baldwin should in no way be read as a rejection of him or his work. He was a man of his times, and he took us an impressively long way toward understanding the alchemy of race and sexuality. His writing gave us many tools for exploring the sexualities of African Americans—a topic that had long been suppressed for reasons of self-protection. I have chosen to investigate his limitations here because a clearer sense of them can help us to unpack the complexity of his insights. Baldwin remained trapped by some of his struggles against homophobia, and he never overcame his deeply ingrained sexism. These limitations— as well as his openness—cost him, because racism and homophobia can injure the spirit and break down the body. By breaking the silence on black homosexuality through his writing, Baldwin both opened possibilities for younger generations of black intellectuals like me and risked losing the love of the very black men whom he so clearly loved.

Conclusion

> The object of one's hatred is never, alas, conveniently outside but is seated in one's lap, stirring in one's bowels and dictating the beat of one's heart. And if one does not know this, one risks becoming an imitation— and, therefore, a continuation—of principles one imagines oneself to despise.
>
> —Baldwin, "Here Be Dragons," 686

During the few short years that James Baldwin taught in western Massachusetts, I often heard him say, "White is a metaphor for safety." It took me a long time to realize that he repeated that line so often because he knew that it was a hard concept to grasp; after all, people were just beginning to talk about whiteness as a constructed identity. The meaning of his phrase lay at the heart of much of what he was about. He wanted us to know that blacks and whites do not have separate histories and that there could be no white people without black people. For Baldwin, whiteness was about a false claim on innocence that depended on the demonization of blackness.

My sense is that Morrison has been greatly influenced by her reading of Baldwin and has taken on a similar project. Both Baldwin and Morrison expose the fragility of whiteness and, in the process, disrupt any notion of pure whiteness, distinct from and in opposition to blackness. Morrison demonstrates that works from this country's master canon that seem to be about whiteness use blackness to construct white identity. Baldwin attacks not only the false binary, white/black but also male/female and heterosexual/homosexual. As we saw previously, according to Baldwin, we all contain "the other—male in female, female in male, white in black and black in white" (1985:690).

Morrison and Baldwin also both critique the ways that black people have been erased from a history that seethed with our presence. And they are concerned with the myths and metaphors of race. Morrison writes about the ways that race establishes difference within our national literature, whereas Baldwin sees whiteness as a metaphor for safety. Although Morrison's work is more developed in her understanding of the way our culture has developed blackness as a figure of speech for the abnormal and evil, Baldwin's work is striking for its early break with race as an essential category. Baldwin often stressed both the destructiveness of and the barriers to insight created by racial categories.

Although both Morrison and Baldwin are impressively attuned to the nuances of black culture, they display a sense of irony that underneath it all we are not so different from white people. Both rely on the unconscious to explain the roots of white racism: White fear and guilt are projected onto black people. The entire nation suffers from white escape from knowledge. Since the unconscious is so closely bound up with sexuality, racial and sexual identity become intimately linked.

The ways that Baldwin and Morrison see the impact of this intertwined relationship differs. Morrison tends to use sexuality as a leverage point of power between unequals. In particular, homosexual behavior becomes a powerful trope for unequal relationships. The scene on the chain gang in *Beloved* (1982) represents this use of homosexuality. The power of the scene comes in part because Morrison almost buries it by focusing on seemingly minor peripheral details. Yet once the reader visualizes the scene, the horror unfolds. Black men are chained together, and every one of them is at the mercy of the guards. Every punishment is a collective punishment. Since death deprives the guards of the use of another black male body, their ultimate punishment of the men in the chain gang becomes not execution but a psychological attack—the invasion of their sexuality and the sense of themselves as men. That the men in the chain gang experience this invasion collectively forces them to bury this secret deep in their (our) cultural psyche. Darieck Scott has come to similar conclusions: "The repressed memory [of African-American men] might also be of the horror of homoerotic domination and desire enacted by and engendered in sexual exploitation" (1999:229).

If Morrison's scene were in the context of an African-American literary culture that recognized a range of male-to-male relationships, from forced to loving, the scene would not contribute to the erasure of black homosexuality. But *Beloved* speaks into a homophobic silence. From Morrison's insights on race, I have been led to ask what intellectual and political feats she has had to perform to erase black queers from her consciousness.

Like Morrison, Baldwin knew that the histories of race and sexuality are inextricably intertwined. Perhaps because Baldwin was more intent on finding space for male homosexual relationships in a hostile environment, he placed greater emphasis on the similarities between the homosexual and the heterosexual. More than Morrison, he was concerned with exposing false binaries: black/white, male/female, gay/straight.

Unfortunately, Baldwin paid a high price for his bravery. And when his manhood—and by extension, his loyalty to the race—was questioned, he did not have an adequate response. His understanding of gender was underdeveloped, and he did not really understand his own insight that "male" and "female" are constructed categories.

Baldwin and Morrison have greatly enriched our understanding of race and sexuality. The boundaries of their understanding provide fertile ground for exploring the way that race and sexuality operate together.

Notes

1. This passage was first brought to my attention in a student paper written by Neeshan Mehretu (1992). I have been influenced by Mehretu's reading of this quoted passage and the one that follows from Morrison's *Beloved*.

2. For an exception, see William S. McFeely's *Frederick Douglass* (1991). McFeely speculates that Edward Covey, a notorious "slave

breaker" in Eastern Shore, Maryland, engaged in frequent homosexual rape of slaves who fell under his power, including Frederick Douglass himself.

3. For a critique of Garber's work, see Reid-Pharr 1993. For a more sensitive view, see Faderman 1991b.

4. For a similar conclusion, see Campbell 1991.

5. I thank Margaret Cerullo and Marla Erlien for helping me see this.

Bibliography

Alarcón, Norma. 1981. "Chicana's Feminist Literature: A Re-vision Through Malintzin/ or Malintzin: Putting Flesh Back on the Object." In *This Bridge Called My Back: Writings by Radical Women of Color,* ed. Cherríe Moraga and Gloria Anzaldúa. Watertown, Mass.: Persephone Press.

Alexander, Elizabeth. 1990. *The Venus Hottentot.* Charlottesville: University Press of Virginia.

Allen, Grant. 1881. "Aesthetic Evolution of Man." *Popular Science Monthly* 21 (January): 342–56.

Allen, Richard. 1970. *Black Awakening in Capitalist America.* Garden City, N.Y.: Anchor Books.

Anzaldúa, Gloria. 1987. *Borderlands/La Frontera: The New Mestizo.* San Francisco: Spinster/Aunt Lute.

Asante, Molefi Kete. 1977. "Editor's Note." *Journal of Black Studies* 8 (2): 123–24.

———. 1987. *The Afrocentric Idea.* Philadelphia: Temple University Press.

Baldwin, James. 1955. *Notes of a Native Son.* Boston: Beacon Press.

———. 1962. *Giovanni's Room.* New York: Dial Press.

———. 1972. *No Name in the Street.* New York: Dial Press.

———. 1979. *Just Above My Head.* New York: Dell Publishing.

———. 1985. "Here Be Dragons." In *The Price of the Ticket: Collected Nonfiction 1948–1985.* New York: St. Martin's Press.

Beale, Frances. 1975. "Slave of a Slave No More: Black Women in Struggle." *Black Scholar* 6 (2): 2–10.

Beer, Gillian. 1983. *Darwin's Plots: Evolutionary Narrative in Darwin, George Elliot, and Nineteenth-Century Fiction.* London: Routledge and Kegan Paul.

Bethel, Lorraine. 1979. "What Chou Mean *We,* White Girl?" *Conditions Five* 2 (2): 86–92.

Blackwell, Emily. 1883. "The Industrial Position of Women." *Popular Science Monthly* 23 (June): 388–99.

Blyden, Edward W. 1878. "Africa and the Africans." *Popular Science Monthly* 27 (September): 385–98.

185

Brewer, Rose M. 1993. "Theorizing Race, Class and Gender: The New Scholarship of Black Feminist Intellectuals and Black Women's Labor." In *Theorizing Black Feminisms: The Visionary Pragmatism of Black Women*, ed. Stanlie M. James and Abena P. A. Busia. London: Routledge.

Brown, Kathleen. 1996. *Good Wives, Nasty Wenches, and Anxious Patriarchs: Gender, Race, and Power in Colonial Virginia*. Chapel Hill: University of North Carolina Press.

Burnham, John C. 1987. *How Superstition Won and Science Lost: Popularizing Science and Health in the United States*. New Brunswick, N.J.: Rutgers University Press.

Cade, Toni, ed. 1970. *The Black Woman: An Anthology*. New York: New American Library.

Campbell, James. 1991. *Talking at the Gates: A Life of James Baldwin*. New York: Viking.

Carby, Hazel V. 1982. "White Woman Listen! Black Feminism and the Boundaries of Sisterhood." In *The Empire Strikes Back: Race and Racism in Seventies Britain*, ed. Centre for Contemporary Cultural Studies. London: Hutchinson.

———. 1985. "'On the Threshold of Woman's Era': Lynching, Empire, and Sexuality in Black Feminist Theory." *Critical Inquiry* 12:262–77.

———. 1986. "It Be's Dat Way Sometime: The Sexual Politics of Women's Blues." *Radical America* 20 (4): 238–49.

———. 1987. *Reconstructing Womanhood: The Emergence of the Afro-American Woman Novelist*. New York: Oxford University Press.

———. 1998. *Race Men*. Cambridge, Mass.: Harvard University Press.

Cell, John W. 1982. *The Highest State of White Supremacy: The Origins of Segregation in South Africa and the American South*. Cambridge, England: Cambridge University Press.

Chanock, Martin. 1982. "Making Customary Law: Men, Women, and Courts in Colonial Northern Rhodesia." In *African Women and the Law: Historical Perspective*, ed. Margaret Jean Hay and Marcia Wright. Boston: Boston University Press.

Chauncey, George. 1994. *Gay New York: Gender, Urban Culture, and the Making of the Gay Male World, 1890–1940*. New York: Basic Books.

Chodorow, Nancy, and Susan Contralto. 1982. "The Fantasy of the Perfect Mother." In *Rethinking the Family: Some Feminist Questions*, ed. Barrie Thorne and Marilyn Yalom. New York: Longman.

Clarke, Cheryl. 1983. "The Failure to Transform: Homophobia in the Black Community." In *Home Girls: A Black Feminist Anthology*, ed. Barbara Smith. Latham, N.Y.: Kitchen Table: Women of Color Press.

————. 1993. "Living the Texts Out: Lesbians and the Uses of Black Women's Traditions." In *Theorizing Black Feminisms: The Visionary Pragmatism of Black Women,* ed. Stanlie M. James and Abena P. A. Busia. London: Routledge.

————. 1999. "Transferences and Confluences: Black Poetries, the Black Arts Movement, and Black Lesbian-Feminism." In *Dangerous Liaisons: Blacks, Gays, and the Struggle for Equality,* ed. Eric Brandt. New York: New Press.

Cleaver, Eldridge. 1968. *Soul on Ice.* New York: Dell Publishing.

Cohen, Cathy J. 1999. *The Boundaries of Blackness: AIDS and the Breakdown of Black Politics.* Chicago: University of Chicago Press.

Cohen, Cathy, and Tamara Jones. 1999. "Fighting Homophobia versus Challenging Heterosexism: 'The Failure to Transform' Revisited." In *Dangerous Liaisons: Blacks and Gays and the Struggle for Equality,* ed. Eric Brandt. New York: New Press.

Coleman, Larry Delano. 1983. "Black Man/Black Woman: Can the Breach Be Healed?" *Nile Review* 2 (7): 5–9.

Collins, Patricia Hill. 1989. "The Social Construction of Black Feminist Thought." *Signs: Journal of Women in Culture and Society* 14 (4): 745–73.

————. 1990. *Black Feminist Thought: Knowledge, Consciousness, and the Politics of Enpowerment.* Boston: Unwin Hyman.

Combahee River Collective. 1981. "A Black Feminist Statement." In *This Bridge Called My Back: Writings by Radical Women of Color,* ed. Cherríe Moraga and Gloria Anzaldúa. Watertown, Mass.: Persephone Press.

Coward, Rosalind. 1983. *Patriarchal Precedents: Sexuality and Social Relations.* London: Routledge and Kegan Paul.

Craighead, James B. 1884. "The Future of the Negro in the South." *Popular Science Monthly* 24 (November): 39–46.

Darwin, Charles. [1859] n.d. *The Origin of the Species by Means of Natural Selection or the Preservation of Favored Races in the Struggle for Life.* Reprint, New York: Modern Library.

————. [1871] n.d. *The Descent of Man and Selection in Relation to Sex.* Reprint, New York: Modern Library.

Davis, Angela Y. 1971. "Reflections on the Black Woman's Role in the Community of Slaves." *Black Scholar* 3 (4): 4–15.

————. 1981. *Women, Race and Class.* New York: Random House.

————. 1998. *Blues Legacies and Black Feminism.* New York: Vintage Books.

Delauney, G. 1881. "Equality and Inequality in Sex." *Popular Science Monthly* 21 (December): 184–92.

De Quatrefages, M.A. 1880. "The Crossing of the Human Races." *Popular Science Monthly* 27 (June): 16–22.

Dill, Bonnie Thornton. 1983. "Race, Class, and Gender: Prospects for an All-Inclusive Sisterhood." *Feminist Studies* 9 (1): 131–50.

Diop, Cheikh Anta. 1974. *The African Origins of Civilization: Myth or Reality.* Trans. Mercer Cook. New York: Lawrence Hill.

Duberman, Martin. 1989. "'Writhing Bedfellows,' in Antebellum South Carolina." In *Hidden from History: Reclaiming the Gay and Lesbian Past,* ed. Martin Duberman, Martha Vincinus, and George Chauncey Jr. New York: New American Library.

Ebron, Paulla A. 1991. "Rapping between Men: Performing Gender." *Radical America* 23 (4): 23–27.

———. 1999. "Tourists as Pilgrims: Commercial Fashioning of Trans-Atlantic Politics." *American Ethnologist.* 26 (4): 910–32.

Edwards, Yoko. 1997. *Politics from a Black Woman's Insides.* Amherst, Mass. Video.

Emerson, Caryl. 1986. "The Outer World and Inner Speech: Bakhtin, Vygotsky and the Internalization of Language." In *Bakhtin: Essays and Dialogues on His Work,* ed. Gary Saul Morson. Chicago: University of Chicago Press.

Evans, Sara. 1979. *Personal Politics.* New York: Vintage Press.

Fabian, Johannes. 1983. *Time and the Other: How Anthropology Makes Its Objects.* New York: Columbia University Press.

Faderman, Lillian. 1991a. "Harlem Nights: Savvy Women of the Twenties Knew Where to Find New York's Lesbian Life." *Advocate* 573: 80–82.

———. 1991b. *Odd Girls and Twilight Lovers: A History of Lesbian Life in Twentieth Century America.* New York: Penguin Books.

Fichmann, Martin. 1984. "Ideological Factors in the Dissemination of Darwinism in England, 1860–1900. In *Transformation and Tradition in the Sciences: Essays in Honor of I. Bernard Cohen,* ed. Everett Mendelsohn. Cambridge, England: Cambridge University Press.

Fiske, John. 1894. *Edward Livingston Youmans: Interpreter of Science to the People.* New York: n.p.

Freud, Sigmund. 1953. *The Standard Edition of the Complete Psychological Works of Sigmund Freud,* trans. and ed. James Stachey, vol. 20. London: Hogarth Press.

Garber, Eric. 1990. "A Spectacle of Color: The Lesbian and Gay Subculture of Jazz Age Harlem." In *Hidden from History: Reclaiming the Gay and Lesbian Past,* ed. Martin Duberman, Martha Vicinus, and George Chauncey Jr. New York: New American Library.

Gates, Henry Louis Jr. 1985. "Introduction: The Language of Slavery." In *The Slave's Narrative,* ed. Charles T. Davis and Henry Louis Gates Jr. Oxford: Oxford University Press.

———. 1999. "Backlash?" In *Dangerous Liaisons: Blacks and Gays and the Struggle for Equality*, ed. Eric Brandt. New York: New Press.

General Accounting Office (GAO). 2000a. GAO Letter Report GAO/GGD-00-38. March 17.

———. 2000b. *U.S. Customs Service: Better Targeting of Airline Passengers for Personal Services Could Produce Better Results*. Washington, D.C.: GAO/GGD-00-38.

Giddings, Paula. 1984. *When and Where I Enter: The Impact of Black Women on Race and Sex in America*. New York: William Morrow Press.

Gilliam, E. W. 1883. "The African in the United States." *Popular Science Monthly* 22 (February): 433–44.

Gilligan, Carol. 1982. *In a Different Voice: Psychological Theory and Women's Development*. Cambridge, Mass.: Harvard University Press.

Gilman, Sander. 1985a. "Black Bodies, White Bodies: Toward an Iconography of Female Sexuality in Late Nineteenth Century Art, Medicine and Literature." *Critical Inquiry* 12 (1): 204–42.

———. 1985b. Preface to *Degeneration: The Darkside of Progress*, ed. Sander Gilman and Edward Chamberlain. New York: Columbia University Press.

———. 1985c. "Sexology, Psychoanalysis and Degeneration: From a Theory of Race to a Race to Theory." In *Degeneration: The Darkside of Progress*, ed. Sander Gilman and Edward Chamberlain. New York: Columbia University Press.

Gilroy, Paul. 1993. *The Black Atlantic: Modernity and Double Consciousness*. Cambridge, Mass.: Harvard University Press.

———. 2000. *Against Race: Imagining Political Culture beyond the Color Line*. Cambridge, Mass.: Belknap Press.

Gould, Stephen Jay. 1981. *The Mismeasure of Man*. New York: W. W. Norton.

Green, Renee. 1994. *"Revue."* Art exhibition. Originally shown at Davis Museum, Wellesley College, Wellesley, Mass.

———. 1996–97. "Partially Buried." Art exhibition. Originally shown at the Pat Hearn Gallery, New York.

Gutman, Herbert. 1977. *The Black Family in Slavery and Freedom*. New York: Vintage Books.

Hammonds, Evelynn. 1986. "Race, Sex, AIDS: The Construction of 'Other.'" *Radical America* 20 (6): 28–36.

Hammonds, Evelynn, and Margaret Cerullo. 1987. "AIDS in Africa: The Western Imagination and the Dark Continent." *Radical America* 21 (2–3): 17–23.

Hare, Nathan, and Julia Hare. 1981. "The Rise of Homosexuality and Other Diverse Alternatives." *Black Male/Female Relationships* 5: 8–15.

Harper, Phillip Brian. 1999. *Private Affairs: Critical Ventures in the Culture of Social Relations*. New York: New York University Press.

Harper-Bolton, Charlyn A. 1982. "A Reconceptualization of the Black Woman." *Black Male/Female Relationships* 6:28–42.

Hayles, N. Katherine. 1999. "Simulating Narratives: What Virtual Creatures Can Teach Us." *Critical Inquiry* 23 (1): 1–26.

Higginbotham, Evelyn Brooks. 1993. *Righteous Discontent: The Women's Movement in the Black Baptist Church, 1880–1920*. Cambridge, Mass.: Harvard University Press.

hooks, bell. 1981. *Ain't I a Woman: Black Women and Feminism*. Boston: South End Press.

———. 1992a. *Black Looks: Race and Representation*. Boston: South End Press.

———. 1992b. "Revolutionary Black Woman." In *Black Looks: Race and Representation*. Boston: South End Press.

———. 1994. *Outlaw Culture: Resisting Representations*. New York: Routledge.

———. 1995. *Art on My Mind: Visual Politics*. New York: New Press.

Hull, Gloria T. 1987. *Color, Sex, and Poetry: Three Women Writers of the Harlem Renaissance*. Bloomington: Indiana University Press.

Jordanova, Ludmilla. 1989. *Sexual Visions: Images of Gender in Science and Medicine between the Eighteenth and Twentieth Centuries*. Madison: University of Wisconsin Press.

Joseph, Gloria I., and Jill Lewis. 1981. *Common Differences*. Garden City, N.Y.: Doubleday.

Karenga, Ron M. 1982. *Introduction to Black Studies*. Los Angeles: Kawaida Publications.

Kousser, J. Morgan. 1974. *The Shaping of Southern Politics: Suffrage Restrictions and the Establishment of the One-Party South, 1880–1910*. New Haven, Conn.: Yale University Press.

Kreitler, G. 1882. "A Curious Burmese Tribe." *Popular Science Monthly* 22 (July): 328–31.

Lawes, W. G. 1882. "Address to Royal Geographical Society by a London Missionary Society Missionary in 1879." *Popular Science Monthly* 22 (July): 328–31.

Lewis, Gordon A. 1883. "Our Marriage and Divorce Laws." *Popular Science Monthly* 23 (June): 224–37.

Lorde, Audre. 1982. *Zami: A New Spelling of My Name*. Trunmansburg, N.Y.: Crossing Press.

———. 1984. *Sister Outsider: Essays and Speeches*. Trunmansburg, N.Y.: Crossing Press.

————. 1988. *A Burst of Light: Essays by Audre Lorde*. Ithaca, N.Y.: Firebrand Books.

Lorde, Audre, and James Baldwin. 1984. "Revolutionary Hope: A Conversation between James Baldwin and Audre Lorde." *Essence* 15 (8): 72–74, 129–30, 133.

Martin, Robert K. 1989. "Knights-Errant and Gothic Seducers: The Representation of Male Friendship in Mid-Nineteenth-Century America." In *Hidden from History: Reclaiming the Gay and Lesbian Past*, ed. Martin Duberman, Martha Vicinus, and George Chauncey Jr. New York: New American Library.

Mbiti, John. 1970. *African Religion and Philosophy*. Garden City, N.Y.: Doubleday.

McCorkle, Susannah. 1997. "Back to Bessie." *American Heritage* 48 (7): 54–71.

McFeely, William S. 1991. *Frederick Douglass*. New York: W. W. Norton.

McLaughlin, Thomas. 1990. "Figurative Language." In *Critical Terms for Literary Study*, ed. Frank Lentricchia and Thomas McLaughlin. Chicago: Chicago University Press.

Mehretu, Neeshan. 1992. "The Representation of Black Women's Sexuality and the Connection of History with Slavery and Lynching." Paper presented for course entitled Race, Sexuality and Representation in U.S. History, Hampshire College, Amherst, Massachusetts.

Moraga, Cherríe. 1983. *Loving in the War Years: lo que nunca pasa por sus labios*. Boston: South End Press.

Moraga, Cherríe, and Gloria Anzaldúa, eds. *This Bridge Called My Back: Writings by Radical Women of Color*. Watertown, Mass.: Persephone Press.

Morrison, Toni. 1982. *Beloved*. New York: Knopf.

————. 1989. "Unspeakable Things Unspoken: The Afro-American Presence in American Literature." *Michigan Quarterly Review* 28 (1): 1–34.

————. 1990. "Marginalization and Contemporary Cultures." In *Discourses: Conversations in Postmodern Art and Culture*, ed. Russell Ferguson. Cambridge, Mass.: MIT Press.

————. 1992a. *Jazz*. New York: Knopf.

————. 1992b. *Playing in the Dark: Whiteness and the Literary Imagination*. Cambridge, Mass.: Harvard University Press.

Mosse, George. 1985. *Nationalism and Sexuality: Respectability and Abnormal Sexuality in Modern Europe*. New York: H. Fertig Publishers.

Mott, Frank Luther. 1938. *A History of American Magazines: 1865–1885*. Vol. 3. Cambridge, Mass.: Harvard University Press.

Mudimbe, V. Y. 1985. *The Invention of Africa: Gnosis, Philosophy, and the Order of Knowledge.* Bloomington: Indiana University Press.

Nobles, Wade. 1974. "Africanity: Its Role in Black Families." *Black Scholar* 5 (9): 19–32.

Nutter, Jeanne D. 2000. *Delaware.* Charleston, S.C.: Arcadia Publishing.

Omolade, Barbara. 1994. *The Rising Song of African American Women.* New York: Routledge.

Palgrave, W. W. 1878. "Malay Life in the Philippines." *Popular Science Monthly* 10 (September): 451–63.

Perkins, Linda M. 1983. "The Impact of the 'Cult of True Womanhood' on the Education of Black Women." *Journal of Social Issues* 39 (3): 17–28.

Pile, Luke Owen. 1872. "Woman and Political Power." *Popular Science Monthly* 4 (May):82–94.

Popular Science Monthly. 1888. Vol. 33 (May).

Radcliffe-Brown, A. R., and Daryll Forde. 1950. *African Systems of Kinship and Marriage.* London: Oxford University Press.

Reagon, Bernice. 1979. "The Borning Struggle: The Civil Rights Movement." In *They Should Have Served That Cup of Coffee,* ed. Dick Cluster. Boston: South End Press.

Reid-Pharr, Robert F. 1993. "The Spectacle of Blackness." *Radical America* 24 (4): 57–65.

Richie, Beth. 1996. *Compelled to Crime: The Gender Entrapment of Battered Black Women.* New York: Routledge.

Richie-Bush, Beth 1983. "Facing Contradictions: Challenge for Black Feminists." *Aegis* 37:14–19.

Said, Edward W. 1978. *Orientalism.* New York: Vintage Books.

Scott, Darieck. 1999. "More Man Than You'll Ever Be: Antonio Fargas, Eldridge Cleaver, and Toni Morrison's *Beloved.*" In *Dangerous Liaisons: Blacks and Gays and the Struggle for Equality,* ed. Eric Brandt. New York: New Press.

Scott, James C. 1985. *Weapons of the Weak: Everyday Forms of Peasant Resistance.* New Haven, Conn.: Yale University Press.

Sedgwick, Eve Kosofsky. 1985. *Between Men: English Literature and Male Homosocial Desire.* New York: Columbia University Press.

Sharpley-Whiting, T. Denean. 1999. *Sexualized Savages, Primal Fears, and Primitive Narratives in French.* Durham, N.C.: Duke University Press.

Shaw, Stephanie. 1996. *What a Woman Ought to Be and to Do: Black Professional Women Workers during the Jim Crow Era.* Chicago: University of Chicago Press.

Smith, Barbara, ed. 1982. *But Some of Us Are Brave.* Old Westbury, N.Y.: Feminist Press.

Spencer, Herbert. 1876. "Comparative Psychology of Man." *Popular Science Monthly* 8 (January): 257–69.

———. 1877. "The Status of Women and Children." *Popular Science Monthly* 9 (March): 433–55.

Spender, Dale. 1983. *Women of Ideas and What Men Have Done to Them: From Aphra Behn to Adrienne Rich.* London: Ark Paperbacks.

Spillers, Hortense J. 1984. "Interstices: A Small Drama of Words." In *Pleasure and Danger: Exploring Sexuality,* ed. Carole Vance. Boston: Routledge and Kegan Paul.

Spurlin, William J. 1999. "Culture, Rhetoric, and Queer Identity: James Baldwin and the Identity Politics of Race and Sexuality." In *Baldwin Now,* ed. Dwight A. McBride. New York: New York University Press.

Steady, Filomina Chioma. 1981. *The Black Woman Cross-Culturally.* Cambridge: Schenkman Publishing.

———. 1987. "African Feminism: A Worldwide Perspective." In *Women in Africa and the African Diaspora,* ed. Rosalyn Terborg-Penn, Andrea Rushing, and Sharon Harley. Washington, D.C.: Howard University Press.

Stepan, Nancy. 1993. "Race and Gender: The Role of Analogy in Science." In *The "Racial" Economy of Science: Toward a Democratic Future,* ed. Sandra Harding. Bloomington: Indiana University Press.

Still, William. [1872] 1968. *The Underground Railroad.* New York: Arno Press.

Stoler, Ann Laura. 1996. *Race and the Education of Desire: Foucault's History of Sexuality and the Colonial Order of Things.* Durham, N.C.: Duke University Press.

Takaki, Ronald T. 1979. *Iron Cages: Race and Culture in Nineteenth-Century America.* Seattle: University of Washington Press.

Terborg-Penn, Rosalyn. 1978. "Discrimination against Afro-American Women in the Women's Movement." In *The Afro-American Woman,* ed. Sharon Harley and Rosalyn Terborg-Penn. New York: Kennikat Press.

Terborg-Penn, Rosalyn, Andrea Rushing, and Sharon Harley, eds. 1987. *Women in Africa and the African Diaspora.* Washington, D.C.: Howard University Press.

Terdiman, Richard. 1985. *Discourse/Counter-Discourse: The Theory and Practice of Symbolic Resistance in Nineteenth Century France.* Ithaca, N.Y.: Cornell University Press.

Thunder Thigh Revue. 1986. "Woman of Substance." Baltimore Theater Project. Performance art.

Van de Warker, Ely. 1875. "Sexual Cerebration." *Popular Science Monthly* 6 (2): 450–64.

Volosinov, V. N. 1973. *Marxism and the Philosophy of Language*. Trans. Ladislav Matejka and I. R. Titunik. New York: Seminar Press.

White, E. Frances. 1983. "Listening to the Voices of Black Feminism." *Radical America* 18 (2–3): 7–25.

———. 1987a. "Civilization Denied: Questions on *Black Athena*." *Radical America* 21 (5): 38–40.

———. 1987b. *Sierra Leone's Settler Women Traders: Women on the Afro European Frontier*. Ann Arbor: University of Michigan Press.

———. 1990. "Africa on My Mind: Gender, Counter Discourse and African-American Nationalism." *Journal of Women's History* 2 (1): 57–73.

White, E. Frances, and Iris Berger. 1999. *Women in Sub-Saharan Africa: Restoring Women to History*. Bloomington: Indiana University Press.

White, Frances Emily. 1875. "Woman's Place in Nature." *Popular Science Monthly* 6 (3): 292–301.

White, Hayden. 1978. *Tropics of Discourse: Essays in Cultural Criticism*. Baltimore: Johns Hopkins University Press.

Wiegman, Robyn. 1995. *American Anatomies: Theorizing Race and Sexuality*. Durham, N.C.: Duke University Press.

Williams, Chancellor. 1974. *Destruction of African Civilization: Great Issues of a Race from 4500 BC to 2000 AD*. Chicago: Third World Press.

Williams, Raymond. 1976. *Keywords: A Vocabulary of Culture and Society*. London: Fontana.

Williamson, Joel. 1974. *The Crucible of Race: Black-White Relations in the American South since Emancipation*. New York: Oxford University Press.

Winthrop, Theodore. 1862. *Cecil Dreeme*. Boston: Ticknor and Fields.

Yanagisako, Sylvia Junko. 1985. *Transforming the Past: Traditions and Kinship among Japanese Americans*. Stanford, Calif.: Stanford University Press.

Yellin, Jean Fagan. 1989. *Women and Sisters: The Antislavery Feminists in American Culture*. New Haven, Conn.: Yale University Press.

Youmans, Edward Livingston. 1881. "Aesthetic Evolution in Man." *Popular Science Monthly* 21 (January): 342–56.

———. 1883a. "Dr. Dix on the Woman Question." 23 (May):120–23.

———. 1883b. "Progress and the Home." *Popular Science Monthly* 23 (June): 412.